GW01337057

The Australian Women's Diary

This diary belongs to ~

DESIGNED BY ROBIN JAMES

Researched and edited by Ariana Klepac

THE AUSTRALIAN WOMEN'S DIARY 1990
First published in Australia in 1989 by
Doubleday, a division of Transworld Publishers (Aust.) Pty Ltd
15-23 Helles Avenue, Moorebank NSW 2170

Copyright © Doubleday 1989

All rights reserved, no part of this publication may be reproduced, stored
in a retrieval system, transmitted in any form or by any means,
electronic, mechanical, photocopying, recording or otherwise without
the prior permission in writing of the publisher.

ISBN 0 86824 391 4
ISSN 0815 130X

Typeset in 9½/11 Cochin Roman by Adtype Photocomposition
Printed in Japan by Dai Nippon
The illustration cover plate by Margaret Preston, *Proteas*, 1925, hand-coloured
woodcut purchased 1976. Collection, Art Gallery of New South Wales

> # The Australian Women's Diary 1990

DOUBLEDAY
Sydney • Auckland • New York • Toronto • London

ACKNOWLEDGEMENTS

The editors and publishers would like to thank the following individuals and associations for their invaluable help with the preparation of this year's diary:

Amanda Beresford, Joanne Birkl, Denise and Rob Blackett, Robyn Christian, Michael Cousens, Marelle Day, Meg Labrum and Amanda Gillespie of the National Film & Sound Archive, Josef Lebovic and the staff of the Josef Lebovic Gallery, Sydney, Mrs E. Orton, Bob Peters, Nina Riemer, Camilla Sandell, the staff of the Mitchell Library, Helen Townsend, Gladys Wells and Susan Wells. As always, a very special thank you to Robin James.

The following gave their permission for copyright material to be included:

Allen & Unwin for extract from *The Life and Times of A Colonial Woman* by Mary Braidwood Mowle, 1854, p.143; Angus & Robertson Publishers for extracts from *The Letters of Rachel Henning*, edited by David Adams, 1979 and extract from *Steak for Breakfast* by Elizabeth O'Connor, 1958 p.143; Arnott's Biscuits Limited for advertisement, p.17; Art Gallery of Western Australia for the painting *Australian Riches* by Kathleen O'Connor, presented by the Art Gallery Society of Western Australia, p.107; Australian Broadcasting Commission for photographs pp.40-1; Australian Consolidated Hosiery for Kayser advertisement, p.121; ICM Australia Pty Ltd for Uncle Toby's advertisement, p.149; the City of Ballarat Fine Art Gallery for E. Phillips Fox painting *The Love Story*, 1903, oil on canvas, Martha Parkinson bequest, 1944, p.115; Colgate-Palmolive for advertisement, p.60; William Collins Pty Ltd for extract from *The Timeless Land* by Eleanor Dark, 1941, p.14; William Collins Pty Ltd and Philippa Poole for extracts from *The Diaries of Ethel Turner* edited by Philippa Poole, 1979, pp.23 & 140; Currency Press for extract from *The Currency Lass*, 1975, p.68; Email Limited for Kelvinator advertisement, p.82; Faulding Family Health for advertisement, p.21; Greenhouse Publications, Melbourne for extract from *Better than Dancing* by Elaine McKenna, 1987, p.57; Pamela Hennessy for the photograph of Janet Waterhouse, p.110; Michael Joseph Ltd for extracts from Maie Casey's *An Australian Story 1857-1907* by Maie Casey, 1962; Kraft Foods Ltd for Bonox advertisement, p.113 and Vegemite advertisement, p.71; La Trobe Library for photograph bottom p.13; Josef Lebovic for the following illustrations: p.7, bottom p.9, p.14, top p.21, p.43, top p.47, top p.67, bottom p.77, both p.91, bottom p.95, p.102, top p.117, p.130 and p.149; Josef Lebovic Gallery for the following illustrations: poster p.29, bottom p.31, top p.55 and John Lewin bird p.55, photographs pp.64-5, bottom p.67; Ellis Rowan p.101, John Lewin p.123, p.125 and top p.147; Lever & Kitchen Pty Ltd for Lux advertisement, p.118; Library Board of Western Australia for photograph, bottom p.93; Mitchell Library for photograph of Mary Grant Bruce, p.81, ball invitation, p.131 and p.143; National Film & Sound Archive for still from *The Cheaters*, p.34; National Library of Australia for paintings by Ellis Rowan p.88, and Louisa Meredith p.89, and photograph of Ellis Rowan, p.137; Nicholas Kiwi (Pacific) Pty Ltd for extracts and illustrations from the *Aspro Year Book*; Penfolds Wines Pty Ltd for advertisements, pp.23 & 87; Penguin Books Australia for extracts from *Ladies Didn't* by Eugénie McNeil and Eugénie Crawford, 1984; Philippa Poole for photograph of Ethel Turner, p.80; Remington Pty Ltd for advertisement, p.95; Royal Agricultural Society of New South Wales for certificate, p.45; Helen Rutledge for extracts from *My Grandfather's House* by Helen Rutledge, 1986; SCECGS Redlands for photograph, p.73; Viking O'Neil for extract from *A Girl at Government House* edited by Helen Vellacott, 1932, p.146; Thea Waddell for the Thea Proctor image on p.141; Wakefield Press for extract from *Arcadian Adelaide* by Thistle Anderson, 1905, p.66; West Australian Newspapers for the photographs at the bottom of p.123; W.D. & H.O. Wills (Australia) Limited for cigarette card, p.87.

In an anthology such as this it is not always possible to acknowledge or even find the copyright holders of certain material. The publishers have made every effort, but apologise in advance for any lapse. They would be pleased to hear from anyone who has not been acknowledged.

Introduction

It is with pleasure that we present our 1990 diary. Our diary is now in its sixth year. As always, we are thankful for your comments and suggestions.

This year's diary reveals some rather intrepid Australian women such as Elizabeth Macarthur and Ellis Rowan, who, despite their lace and long skirts, showed great perseverance and devotion in their endeavours. Also included are some of Australia's notorious women, remembered for their being intrepid in the face of the law!

This year we have added a visitors' page so that your guests' names and special occasions can be recorded.

Of course, the usual potpourri of memoirs, recipes, eccentric advice and 'helpful' hints has been collected for your enjoyment and, as always, there are the special days and school holidays.

Best wishes for 1990 and may you have many happy events to record in your diary.

The Editors

New Year

THE BOOK OF THE NEW YEAR

With this number we enter on the first month of a new year.

The last page of the year 1894 has now been closed forever, and the book of the new year is open before us. What a record it may bear for us all, whether joy or sorrow, progress or slipping backward, hopes and ambitions realized, or fears fulfilled, it is impossible for any of us to say, and it is well for us that it is so.

But let us instead of looking forward, look backward for a little, and in comparing the present with the past we shall see good reason for hope in the future, especially from a woman's point of view. Those who have the cause of women at heart cannot but rejoice at the progress which has taken place, especially in Australasia. Not only has New Zealand recognised that the political disability of women has no reasonable basis, but South Australia has followed in her wake, and proclaimed the absolute equality of the sexes in the election of those who are to rule her people.

On all sides there is a growing sense of a woman's influence in all departments of life, and a realization that the qualities which purify and beautify a home are capable of a wider and fuller expansion beyond the narrower limits to which they have hitherto been confined.

The Dawn, 1 January 1895

NEW YEAR OFF THE CAPE OF GOOD HOPE

Nothing particular happened since Christmas, until New Year's Day. On New Year's Eve there was a grand dress concert, given in the single men's apartments. A large bill was posted up just as it would be at home announcing the concert. However I couldn't go. Fred had knocked his leg again, and he went to bed. But for the sake of old times I stayed up with a few others, who were in a similar fix. About 11.30 the cannon was fired, and that continued until after 12. Then there were fireworks, ringing the bells, dancing and singing. It was all high day again for a time, then a few hours quiet, and all was astir again with their puddings. It was pretty much the same as Christmas Day, very rough and raining all day, and everybody was agreeable except the woman in the next berth to me – and she is a disagreeable thing – but I don't say much more to her than I am obliged. I can get on with every one else very well.

Anna Cook, on board the *Scottish Hero*, off the Cape of Good Hope, 1883

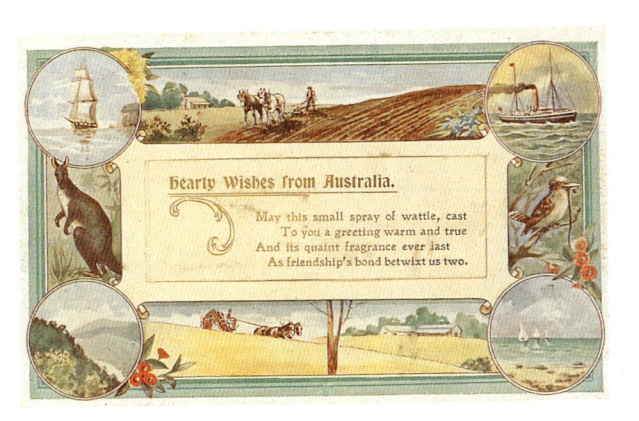

HAPPY NEW YEAR

Monday. Margaret was the first to wish me a *happy New Year!* I am determined on not grumbling this year, *if* I can avoid it – and so I trust myself, that it may be happy!

I have begun it by doing all that I most dislike, on purpose to try and improve my temper – for they tell me, I'm altered for the worse in this respect – Oh! who would not in my case?

Annie Baxter, 1 January 1844

Leaves from a January Notebook

On New Year's Day we were all up very early, having arranged to walk to the sandy flat off the beach road to get native flowers. Mr Hugh Mackay went with us and Margaret – only fancy Margaret! She tried to escape but could not. Mrs Haloran, of course, hastened to open the gate and wish us many happy new years, adding, 'Ye'll have a fine bogie (bathe) this morning.' So we told Mr Hugh he had been promoted, as he was now a Companion of the Bath! We got a great many fine blandfordias and some ipomoeas, and got home in time to arrange flowers for the library and decorate the breakfast table...

Mrs M'Leod, Miss Marion, and Hector arrived at four o'clock to dine and stayed all night...We were a party of sixteen. Afterwards we danced, first on the lawn and then in what was the pink room, but is now our dancing and recreation room.

Annabella Boswell's Journal, 1844

January

MONDAY 1

New Year's Day
Festival of Sydney begins
1901 Federation of the Commonwealth of Australia

TUESDAY 2

1822 Agricultural society formed in Tas.
1856 Name 'Tasmania' replaced 'Van Diemen's Land'
1914 b. Vivian Stuart (William Stuart Long), author of *The Australians* ser

WEDNESDAY 3

1870 b. writer, Henry Handel Richardson (Ethel Florence Lindesay Richardson), author of *The Getting of Wisdom*
1944 b. writer, Blanche d' Alpuget, author of *Turtle Beach*
1948 b. Lady 'Kanga' Tryon, Baroness Tryon of Durnford

THURSDAY 4

First quarter of the moon 8.40 pm EST
1688 William Dampier sighted the north-west coast of 'New Holland'

FRIDAY 5

Twelfth Night
1932 Aviatrix Lores Bonney flew 1600 km from Brisbane to Wangaratta, in one day

SATURDAY 6

1797 b. Elizabeth Mitchell, pioneer pastoralist and a descendant of the French nobility who escaped the French Revolution
1819 b. feminist, Caroline Dexter

SUNDAY 7

Epiphany
1788 First Fleet sighted Tas.
1941 The Argonauts Club for children began on ABC radio

	January					
M	T	W	T	F	S	S
1	2	3	4	5	6	7
8	9	10	11	12	13	14
15	16	17	18	19	20	21
22	23	24	25	26	27	28
29	30	31				

EVENING ON THE HAWKESBURY.

TABLE DECORATIONS FOR EVERY OCCASION

The art of table decoration is one that should have the consideration of every hostess for the pleasure to one's guests is always greatly enhanced by the treatment of the decorative scheme...

For a simple dinner party a floating flower bowl, with one or two choice specimen flowers makes a pleasing feature, otherwise a small dainty basket, silver gilt with perhaps a few specimen roses artistically arranged in same, makes a charming centre-piece.

A brown basket of the Japanese type with perhaps a few pretty yellow toned flowers carelessly lying in same is also effective.

For novelty table decorations there are many pleasing schemes that could be undertaken.

For a farewell party a floral centre-piece in the form of a ship, horse-shoe or swastika, is always appreciated by one's guests.

For a children's party, a bon-bon in flowers with ribbons from each end taken to each guest's plate with a dainty posy as a finishing touch, or a little gift is always something that brings joy to the hearts of children.

For a wedding table decoration, a wedding-bell or horse-shoe could be suspended from the ceiling at a fair height above the table, and from the bell ribbons tied in a narrow width either in white, pink, lemon or silver forms a pleasing and novel feature.

In the foregoing we have only outlined just a few schemes that are not in any way difficult to carry out, and decorations of tables is so fascinating a subject that one could, should space permit, give quite a number of further suggestions.

Searl's Key to Australian Gardening, 1922

January

MONDAY 8

Baptism of the Lord
1878 First public demonstration of the telephone in Australia, in Elizabeth Street, Melbourne

TUESDAY 9

1868 Last convicts arrived in WA
1905 Women granted the vote in Qld

WEDNESDAY 10

1696 Vlamingh discovered the Swan River at the site of present day Perth
1870 Victorian Academy of Arts founded
1929 First public demonstration of television in Australia, in Melbourne

THURSDAY 11

Full moon 2.57 pm EST
1911 b. painter, Nora Heysen

FRIDAY 12

1836 Charles Darwin arrived in Sydney on the HMS *Beagle*
1986 Gateway Bridge opened in Brisbane

SATURDAY 13

1939 'Black Friday' bushfires in Vic. raged from the Grampian Ranges to Gippsland

SUNDAY 14

1958 Qantas began its round-the-world air service
1968 d. poet, Dorothea Mackellar who wrote the poem 'My Country' when she was 19

		January				
M	T	W	T	F	S	S
1	2	3	4	5	6	7
8	9	10	11	12	13	14
15	16	17	18	19	20	21
22	23	24	25	26	27	28
29	30	31				

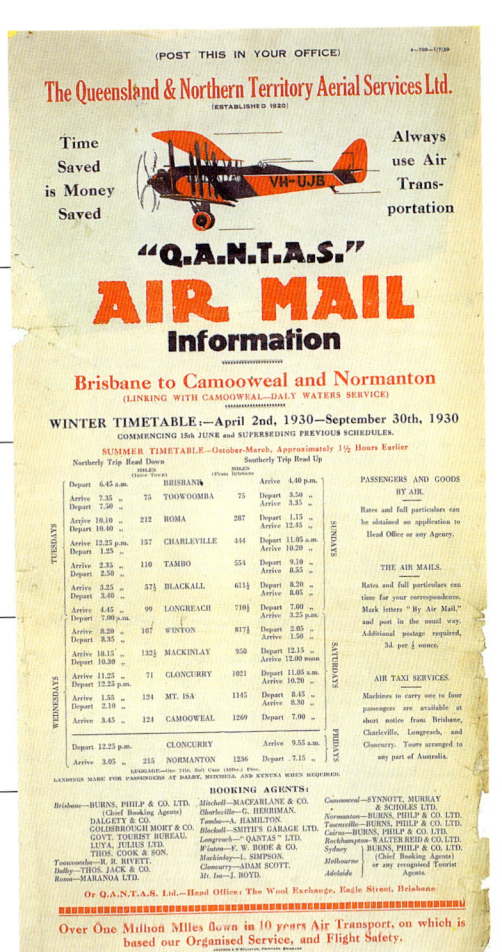

(POST THIS IN YOUR OFFICE)

The Queensland & Northern Territory Aerial Services Ltd.
(ESTABLISHED 1920)

Time Saved is Money Saved

Always use Air Transportation

"Q.A.N.T.A.S."
AIR MAIL Information

Brisbane to Camooweal and Normanton
(LINKING WITH CAMOOWEAL—DALY WATERS SERVICE)

WINTER TIMETABLE:—April 2nd, 1930—September 30th, 1930
COMMENCING 15th JUNE and SUPERSEDING PREVIOUS SCHEDULES.

SUMMER TIMETABLE—October-March, Approximately 1½ Hours Earlier

Northerly Trip Read Down				Southerly Trip Read Up	
	MILES (Inter Town)		MILES (From Brisbane)		
Depart 6.45 a.m.		BRISBANE		Arrive 4.40 p.m.	
Arrive 7.35 " Depart 7.50 "	75	TOOWOOMBA	75	Depart 3.50 " Arrive 3.35 "	TUESDAYS
Arrive 10.10 " Depart 10.40 "	212	ROMA	287	Depart 1.15 " Arrive 12.45 "	
Arrive 12.25 p.m. Depart 1.25 "	157	CHARLEVILLE	444	Depart 11.05 a.m. Arrive 10.20 "	SUNDAYS
Arrive 2.35 " Depart 2.50 "	110	TAMBO	554	Depart 9.10 " Arrive 8.55 "	
Arrive 3.25 " Depart 3.40 "	57½	BLACKALL	611½	Depart 8.20 " Arrive 8.05 "	
Arrive 4.45 " Depart 7.00 p.m.	99	LONGREACH	710½	Depart 7.00 " Arrive 3.25 p.m.	
Arrive 8.20 " Depart 8.35 "	107	WINTON	817½	Depart 2.05 " Arrive 1.50 "	SATURDAYS
Arrive 10.15 " Depart 10.30 "	132½	MACKINLAY	950	Depart 12.15 " Arrive 12.00 noon	
Arrive 11.25 " Depart 12.25 p.m.	71	CLONCURRY	1021	Depart 11.05 a.m. Arrive 10.20 "	WEDNESDAYS
Arrive 1.55 " Depart 2.10 "	124	MT. ISA	1145	Depart 8.45 " Arrive 8.30 "	
Arrive 3.45 "	124	CAMOOWEAL	1269	Depart 7.00 "	FRIDAYS
Depart 12.25 p.m.		CLONCURRY		Arrive 9.55 a.m.	
Arrive 3.05 "	215	NORMANTON	1236	Depart 7.15 "	

LUGGAGE—One 11lb. Suit Case (16lb=.) Free.
LANDINGS MADE FOR PASSENGERS AT DALBY, MUNGALLA AND KYEUNA WHEN REQUIRED.

PASSENGERS AND GOODS BY AIR.
Rates and full particulars can be obtained on application to Head Office or any Agency.

THE AIR MAILS.
Rates and full particulars can time for your correspondence. Mark letters "By Air Mail," and post in the usual way. Additional postage required, 3d. per ½ ounce.

AIR TAXI SERVICES.
Machines to carry one to four passengers are available at short notice from Brisbane, Charleville, Longreach, and Cloncurry. Tours arranged to any part of Australia.

BOOKING AGENTS:

Brisbane—BURNS, PHILP & CO. LTD. (Chief Booking Agents)
DALGETY & CO.
GOLDSBROUGH MORT & CO.
GOVT. TOURIST BUREAU.
LUYA, JULIUS LTD.
THOS. COOK & SON.
Toowoomba—H. R. RIVETT.
Dalby—THOS. JACK & CO.
Roma—MARANOA LTD.
Mitchell—MACFARLANE & CO.
Charleville—G. HERRIMAN.
Tambo—A. HAMILTON.
Blackall—SMITH'S GARAGE LTD.
Longreach—"QANTAS" LTD.
Winton—F. W. BODE & CO.
Mackinlay—L. SIMPSON.
Cloncurry—ADAM SCOTT.
Mt. Isa—J. BOYD.
Camooweal—SYNNOTT, MURRAY & SCHOLES LTD.
Normanton—BURNS, PHILP & CO. LTD.
Townsville—BURNS, PHILP & CO. LTD.
Cairns—BURNS, PHILP & CO. LTD.
Rockhampton—WALTER REID & CO. LTD.
Sydney—BURNS, PHILP & CO. LTD. (Chief Booking Agents)
Melbourne—or any recognised Tourist Agents.
Adelaide—

Or Q.A.N.T.A.S. Ltd.—Head Office: The Wool Exchange, Eagle Street, Brisbane

Over One Million Miles flown in 10 years Air Transport, on which is based our Organised Service, and Flight Safety.

January

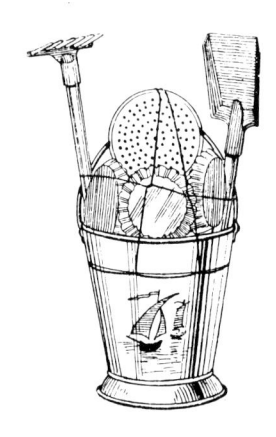

ON A SUMMER'S DAY

Picnics were our great pleasure and there were many of them. Sometimes there would be two or three hired horse-buses and whole crowds of us would go off, children on top and grown-ups inside, perhaps to Maroubra which had the added attraction of the wreck of the *Hereward*, or to The Spit, both favourite places and a lovely day would be spent with the sun, sea and sand.

The best picnics though were those in a large launch called the *Swan*: we would go to some beach where practically by magic, there would be fishermen drawing a net. That really was exciting. I don't think we ever ate the fish, but potatoes boiled in seawater had, we were sure, a different and much better flavour than usual.

Later, when we were grown-up, National Park was the place. We used to go by train, from Redfern at 8 am. It doesn't sound like fun, but it was. We had a reserved carriage called a Saloon to Sutherland and walked down to the River where boats would be waiting for us and rowed up to the selected place for lunch. It was always a lovely day and the wattle out and some delectable flowers with the elegant name of Stinking Roger. After lunch, the thing to do was to go and look for lyrebirds but I don't think anyone ever saw one.

Helen Rutledge, *My Grandfather's House*, 1986

MONDAY 15

1842 b. Sister Mary McKillop
1913 b. pianist and composer, Miriam Hyde
1975 *Lake Illawarra* – Tasman Bridge disaster in Hobart

TUESDAY 16

1793 First free settlers arrived in Sydney on the *Bellona*
1796 Australia's first theatre opened in Bligh Street, Sydney

WEDNESDAY 17

1861 d. dancer and courtesan, Lola Montez, mistress of Alexandre Dumas, Franz Liszt and King Ludwig of Bavaria
1877 b. May Gibbs, author of *Snugglepot and Cuddlepie*
1942 b. journalist and media personality, Ita Buttrose

THURSDAY 18

1788 Governor Arthur Phillip first entered Botany Bay
1815 First school for Aboriginal people opened in Parramatta

FRIDAY 19

Last quarter of the moon 7.17 am EST
1970 Metric measurements introduced

SATURDAY 20

1983 d. author, painter, publisher and pilot, Lady Maie Casey

SUNDAY 21

St Agnes' Day
1788 Governor Phillip first entered Port Jackson and landed at Camp Cove
1815 First road over the Blue Mountains completed
1899 b. writer, Ernestine Hill, author of *My Love Must Wait*

	January					
M	T	W	T	F	S	S
1	2	3	4	5	6	7
8	9	10	11	12	13	14
15	16	17	18	19	20	21
22	23	24	25	26	27	28
29	30	31				

Australia Day

BARANGAROO

Now the white men, accompanied by Nanbarree and Booron, were landing. Aie! how ugly they were! They were coming forward, nodding, smiling, holding out their gifts as usual, and Bennilong was, also as usual, growing noisy and assertive in his excitement.

Barangaroo thrust her lower lip out and made a contemptuous noise. It was food which they were offering, and there was some of the strange drink, too, which Bennilong was always talking about. It was a magic drink, he said, which brought men strength and wisdom and ecstasy, and he had told her that he believed it to be by virtue of this drink alone that the Bereewolgal acquired their power. Barangaroo was prepared to believe anything of the white men, but she was not prepared to admit that her own people needed any greater strength than was already theirs, any deeper wisdom than that which their ancestors had bequeathed to them in their Law, any sweeter ecstasies than those provided by their tribal rites, by courtship and mating, by parenthood, by life itself.

Eleanor Dark, *The Timeless Land*, 1941

HORRORS OF THE PASSAGE

Without a hope of relief, I was fain to content myself within the narrow limits of a wretched cabin, for to add to the horrors of the common passage to the deck, Captain Nepean ordered it to be made a hospital for the sick, the consequence of which was that I never left my cabin till I finally quitted the ship. Thus precluded from the general advantages that even the convicts enjoyed – air and exercise – no language can express, no imagination conceive the misery I experienced. Approaching near the equator (where the heat in the best of situations is almost insupportable) assailed with noisome stenches, that even in the cold of an English winter, hourly effusions of oil of tar in my cabin could not dispel, two sides of it surrounded with wretches whose dreadful imprecations and shocking discourses ever rang in my distracted ears, a sickly infant constantly claiming maternal cares, my spirits failing, my health forsaking me, nothing but the speedy change which took place, could have prevented me from falling a helpless victim to the unheard of inhumanity of a set of monsters whose triumph and pleasure seemed to consist in aggravating my distress. To a person unacquainted with the innumerable insults and cruelties I was necessitated to bear with, this may appear the language of passion, resentment, or of heart, desiring revenge, but it will be admitted to be the conclusions of truth and of justice when it is known in addition the wrongs I have already recited that we were deprived of a part of our little ration, and insultingly told we should have less if they thought proper...

Elizabeth Macarthur on board
the *Neptune*, 1789

The Aquarius Birthday
20 JANUARY – 18 FEBRUARY

The symbol for Aquarius is a man pouring water from a jar, but although he is the water-bearer, remember that Aquarius is an airy sign. Aquarius rules the legs below the knee, and the ankles. This sign corresponds to the eleventh house of the horoscope, which stands for friendships, hopes and wishes. You can pick Aquarians more easily by their character than by appearance, for this is the sign of man himself. Aquarians are very normal in appearance, sometimes inclined to full figure.

Aquarians are friendly to all, great humanitarians, and get easily into touch with the fellow humans and with strangers. The Aquarius word is 'What!' the motto 'Fellowship.'

Aspro Year Book, 1936

THE YEAR OF THE HORSE

The year 1990 is the year of the Horse in the Chinese calendar. If you were born in 1906, 1918, 1930, 1942, 1954, 1966 or 1978, then this is your year.

Those people born in the year of the Horse are gentle and helpful. They try their best to help other people with their tasks even though they themselves will not reap any rewards from it. They must be careful as often their characters make them vulnerable to manipulation by others, and they may be used for others' purposes. However, they make valuable and indispensable friends to many people. Those born under the sign of the Horse will find harmony if they marry those born in the year of the Tiger, Sheep or Dog, but will have trouble with those of the Rat, Ox or Horse.

January

MONDAY 22
1787 British Parliament announced that a penal colony was to be founded in Australia
1853 University of Melbourne opened
1875 b. zoologist and philanthropist, Dr Georgina Sweet

TUESDAY 23
1786 King George III announced his plan to send convicts to a land in the southern hemisphere

WEDNESDAY 24
1788 French explorer Jean la Perouse arrived at Botany Bay, just six days after Governor Phillip
1872 b. writer, Ethel Turner, author of *Seven Little Australians*
1946 b. actress, Helen Morse

THURSDAY 25

FRIDAY 26
Australia Day, holiday NT, NSW, Qld, ACT
1788 Foundation of NSW
1798 First sighting of a lyrebird at Bargo, NSW
1958 Darwin proclaimed a city

SATURDAY 27
New moon 5.20 am EST
Chinese New Year of the Horse

SUNDAY 28
1875 b. actress and author, Ethel Kelly

	January					
M	T	W	T	F	S	S
1	2	3	4	5	6	7
8	9	10	11	12	13	14
15	16	17	18	19	20	21
22	23	24	25	26	27	28
29	30	31				

Leaves from a February Notebook

Oh, my dear A., what shall we do? Do not be alarmed – it is only that the thermometer was at 106° at ten this morning in our coolest spot. It is nearly two, but I cannot summon up courage to go and look again, because I have to meet this sirocco in getting to it; and it really glues up my skin and takes away my breath. Moreover, we can scarcely see to do anything (and it is always better to do something, since it occupies the mind and prevents one feeling so very hot), because here is one constant cloud of dust passing through the air, as it might be drifting snow, or rather driving snow; but oh, how different in appearance and feeling! Were it snow, we might complain of the cold; but then, how we should enjoy the great roaring fire! [1851]

A. de Q. Robin (ed.) *Australian Sketches, the Journals and Letters of Frances Perry*, 1984

HOW TO RESTORE A BLACK DRESS

If the dress is of cashmere or merino, and good enough to re-make, proceed as follows: Unpick it carefully and brush each width separately until free from dust. If there are any grease spots, remove them by applying a little turpentine or benzine. Then lay the pieces upon a table, and sponge both sides with soft water as hot as the hand can bear. Lay singly over a clothes' horse until nearly dry, then iron on the wrong side (with black material laid underneath) with a fairly hot iron. If these very simple instructions are followed, the material will look almost as good as new.

The Dawn, February 1895

January February

MONDAY 29

Australia Day holiday WA, SA, Vic., Tas.
1840 New Zealand founded
1939 b. feminist, Germaine Greer, author of *The Female Eunuch*
1945 b. concert pianist, Diana Weeks

TUESDAY 30

1882 b. racing motorist, Nina Jones
1854 Cobb & Co began coach services between Castlemaine, Bendigo and Melbourne
1931 b. writer, Shirley Hazzard, author of *The Transit of Venus*

WEDNESDAY 31

Festival of Sydney ends
1880 The *Bulletin* first published
1912 Contest to find a design for Canberra closed. It was won by Walter Burley Griffin

THURSDAY 1

St Brigid of Ireland's Day
1948 d. founding member of the CWA, Ruth Fairfax
1984 Medicare Health Scheme introduced

FRIDAY 2

Candlemas Day
1803 Yarra River discovered

SATURDAY 3

First quarter of the moon 4.32 am EST
1954 Queen Elizabeth II began the first tour of Australia by a reigning monarch

SUNDAY 4

	February					
M	T	W	T	F	S	S
				1	2	3	4
5	6	7	8	9	10	11
12	13	14	15	16	17	18
19	20	21	22	23	24	25
26	27	28				

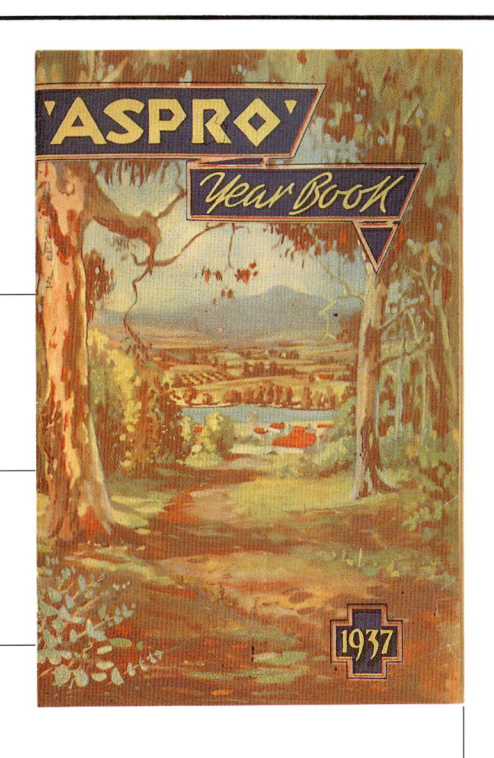

February

COMPLEXION SUICIDE

Vanishing creams are not as harmful as they are suspected to be if they are used with discretion. It would be complexion suicide to go to bed without a thorough cleansing of the face. It is also dangerous to apply cream and powder during the day on top of dirt. Dressing rooms on railway stations and in the big shops show us altogether too much of this evil. A woman will rush in, hot and dusty. She extracts her jar of vanishing cream from her bag. It is followed by powder and a big puff, far from clean. A handful of cream is hastily scrubbed into the already laden pores of her face, that is followed by blobs of powder levelled off with the puff. And when she reaches her forty-fifth birthday her friends wonder why she looks like a dissipated denizen of the underworld. It is a sad story.

Helen's Weekly, November 1927

. . .

A TIMELY TABLE

The following table gives the length of time required for cooking fruit:

Grapes and cherries, five minutes.
Currants, blackberries, raspberries, six to eight minutes.
Gooseberries and halved peaches, ten minutes.
Strawberries, fifteen minutes.
Whole peaches, twenty minutes.
Halved pears and quinces, twenty minutes.
Sliced pineapple, twenty minutes.
Crab apples and sliced pears, thirty minutes.

The Dawn, February 1895

MONDAY 5

1941 Women's Auxiliary Australian Air Force (WAAAF) formed

TUESDAY 6

1952 Accession of Queen Elizabeth II
1986 Mary Gaudron, first woman judge appointed to the High Court

WEDNESDAY 7

1788 Colony of NSW formally proclaimed
1896 Constance Stone registered as first woman doctor in Melbourne
1986 Lindy Chamberlain released from jail

THURSDAY 8

1918 b. co-author of *The Billings Method*, Evelyn Livingston Billings
1928 b. writer, Elizabeth Harrower, author of *The Long Prospect*
1976 d. singer, Gladys Moncrieff

FRIDAY 9

1856 d. pioneer, Elizabeth Macarthur
1986 Eight women ordained as Australia's first women deacons at a ceremony at St Paul's, Melbourne

SATURDAY 10

Full moon 5.16 am EST
Total lunar eclipse at 5.12 am (EST) visible from all around Australia
1897 b. actress, Dame Judith Anderson
1898 b. dramatic soprano, Marjorie Lawrence

SUNDAY 11

1788 First court sat at Sydney Cove
1861 Burke and Wills reached the Gulf of Carpentaria
1986 Joan Child became first woman Speaker of the House of Representatives

February

M	T	W	T	F	S	S
			1	2	3	4
5	6	7	8	9	10	11
12	13	14	15	16	17	18
19	20	21	22	23	24	25
26	27	28				

St Valentine's Day

FOR YOUNG PEOPLE AND LOVERS

Don't try to win love by flattery.

Don't allow yourself to be won in that way.

Don't try to buy love by rich and numerous gifts; love got in that way is not worth the having, for it is not love at all.

Don't take anybody who comes along and offers himself, through fear that there may not be another chance. Infinitely better a single life than a married existence full of wretchedness and misery.

Don't marry for physical beauty alone; for unless mated with beauty of mind and spirit, it is truly an apple of ashes.

The Dawn, February 1895

AN ENGAGING PASTIME

Another thing to do was to get engaged. Our Mother knew a young lady who announced her engagement on returning from a row. The fiance, who looked slightly dazed, was supposed to have confided to a friend that he must have bumped his head when he caught that crab, as he could remember nothing about it.

Helen Rutledge, *My Grandfather's House*, 1986

THE COURSE OF TRUE LOVE

The romance between Ethel Turner and Herbert Curlewis suffered many setbacks. Ethel repeatedly rejected Curlewis who, even so, remained patient and devoted. Once they became engaged in 1891, Ethel had to keep the engagement secret for five years from her tyrannical stepfather, and carry on a furtive relationship with Herbert. The following excerpts taken from Ethel's diary, prove that the course of true love never did run smoothly.

6 March [1891]: This morning there was a letter from C... He is going to send back all the letters I have written...Mr Creed handed me a parcel from C. I went and opened it and there were every single letter I had ever written since Jan. 1889 – 18 in all, answers to invitations and such mostly. Also all the programmes at dances with my name on. Also two withered roses and the little verse book and card I sent at Xmas to him – And there endeth the last chapter.

17 March: I was talking to Mr Creed in our drawing room and asking him some quotations, at same time I asked him 2 words of Greek that were in an envelope C. sent back, I said I had come across them in reading – he said 'I will ask Curlewis' – it couldn't have been worse.

18 March: Did some shopping – at tram C. came up and shook hands, I felt quite angry, he said, 'have you been asking Creed for any more Greek?' – I hate them both.

26 April: Louie...says C. was awfully miserable last night and confided in her – she says he cried – great dry sobs...Oh, I do feel a wretch and yet I can't like him if I can't, it is a miserable affair altogether...it does seem too bad of me.

Kiss, kiss away, and pray don't be shy, Only the man in the moon is nigh!

9 May: Curlewis, Sid and Pickburn had been sailing and came home for tea, I hardly spoke to former. I had to let him bring me home though and...I can't write it down. Lay awake nearly all night.

22 October: C. came up by 10.15 am train...He has some trouble I fancy, he seemed older and graver but said he wouldn't tell me cause he only wanted to think of pleasant things all day. It was lovely being together all day. I am so glad he loves me as he does. Love is even more beautiful, more infinite than the poets say and Life is very beautiful.

Philippa Poole (ed.), *The Diaries of Ethel Turner,* 1979

MAYBANKE SUSANNAH ANDERSON

Born in Surrey, England, in 1845, Maybanke Anderson travelled to Australia with her parents in 1854. While she was training to become a teacher, her father left the family. In 1867 she married a timber merchant who deserted her in 1884 after becoming a drunkard. Undaunted, she opened Maybanke College for young ladies which soon acquired a strong reputation. In 1893, due to recent legislation which included desertion as grounds for divorce, she was able to free herself from her husband.

Maybanke Anderson was a strong advocate of equality for women and in the 1880s became involved in the suffragette movement. Like others in the movement, she wished the age of consent to be raised and reviled society's double moral standards for men and women. She was president of the Womanhood Suffrage League of New South Wales from 1893-1896. She was also a member of an intellectual feminist group, the Women's Literary Society, founder of the Home Reading Union, an office-holder for the University of Sydney Women's Society, involved in the Kindergarten Union of New South Wales and editor of the *Woman's Voice*, her own fortnightly paper. In 1897 she was appointed first registrar of the Teacher's Central Registry.

Maybanke Anderson wrote numerous articles for the press on subjects as diverse as travel, politics and jumble sales, and pamphlets on the history of Pittwater and Hunters Hill. Although wary of the undesirable influence of the cinema, she was keen to promote good educational films, and also Australian films.

Maybanke Anderson died in Paris in 1927 during a trip to Europe.

February

MONDAY 12

1793 John Macarthur received land grant on which he built Elizabeth Farm House (named after his wife, Elizabeth Macarthur), the oldest surviving building in Australia
1959 b. actress, Sigrid Thornton

TUESDAY 13

Regatta Day, Tas.
1913 University of Western Australia opened
1936 b. poet and critic, Judith Rodriguez
1938 b. botanical artist, Rosa Fiveash

WEDNESDAY 14

St Valentine's Day
1779 d. Captain James Cook, speared to death by natives in the Sandwich
1966 Decimal currency introduced
1975 Order of Australia honours introduced

THURSDAY 15

1898 d. women's health reform campaigner, Brettena Smyth
1942 Japanese captured Singapore, 15,384 Australians troops imprisoned
1954 Queen Elizabeth II opened Federal Parliament in Canberra

FRIDAY 16

Festival of Perth begins
1845 b. feminist and teacher, Maybanke Susannah Anderson
1983 Ash Wednesday fires in Vic. and SA

SATURDAY 17

1788 Lord Howe Island discovered
1848 b. writer and founder of the *Dawn*, Louisa Lawson
1931 North and south halves of the Sydney Harbour Bridge joined

SUNDAY 18

Last quarter of the moon 4.48 am EST
1793 First school established in Sydney
1911 First Australian bush nurse, Mary Thompson, took up her post in Beech Forest, Vic.

			February			
M	T	W	T	F	S	S
			1	2	3	4
5	6	7	8	9	10	11
12	13	14	15	16	17	18
19	20	21	22	23	24	25
26	27	28				

The Pisces Birthday
19 FEBRUARY – 20 MARCH

The symbol for Pisces is the pair of fishes swimming in opposite directions, but tied together by their tails. Pisces rules the feet in the human body, and this sign of the Zodiac corresponds to the twelfth and last house of the horoscope, which rules the hidden side of things. You can usually pick a Pisces native easily. They fall into two main groups. One is slight in build, maybe even thin, with a beautiful pale or delicate skin and complexion, fairish hair, or dark, soft and fine. This type is often very pretty. The other type is bulky and fleshy, with short legs, weak bones, and narrow chest, large, fleshy face, big mouth, low, wide forehead, watery, weak-looking, or very full eyes, and a rolling, lurching, clumsy walk.

The Pisces word is 'Perhaps', and the motto 'Sympathy'. The weak part of the anatomy is the feet, and complaints are chest afflictions and bunions.

The Aspro Year Book, 1936

A FEW DON'TS

Don't wear a fur boa with a muslin gown.

Don't put a smart new jacket over an old shabby skirt.

Don't mix furs – such as a sable throatlet and astrachan revers.

Don't let your petticoat clash with your dress in color.

Don't carry your gloves in your hand – put them on before leaving the house.

Don't forget that a really well-dressed woman should be, to all appearance, perfectly unconscious of the favorable impression that she creates.

The Dawn, March 1895

February

MONDAY 19
1942 Darwin bombed
1942 Kindergarten of the Air began in WA
1951 Jean Lee became first woman to be hanged in Australia since 1894

TUESDAY 20
1861 b. writer and traveller, Mary Gaunt, author of *Kirkham's Find*
1906 b. artist, Constance Stokes
1913 b. writer, Dame Mary Durack, author of *Kings in Grass Castles*

WEDNESDAY 21

THURSDAY 22
1791 First land grant of 30 acres issued to James Ruse at Parramatta

FRIDAY 23
Royal Canberra Show begins
1890 b. producer and Australia's first film star, Lottie Lyell
1931 d. opera singer, Dame Nellie Melba (Helen Porter Armstrong)
1975 Saturday post deliveries abolished

SATURDAY 24
1867 b. nurse and poet, Grace Carmichael
1948 b. ACTU advocate, Jan Marsh
1961 Three women began their training as the NT's first policewomen

SUNDAY 25
New moon 6.54 pm EST
Royal Canberra Show ends
1834 b. naturalist and writer, Caroline Atkinson
1961 Last tram ran in Sydney

		February				
M	T	W	T	F	S	S
			1	2	3	4
5	6	7	8	9	10	11
12	13	14	15	16	17	18
19	20	21	22	23	24	25
26	27	28				

Pioneering Women

ELIZABETH MACARTHUR

Elizabeth Macarthur was one of the first intelligent and cultivated women to arrive in the colony and her company was much sought after. Three years after her arrival with her husband Lieutenant John Macarthur in 1793, Macarthur was granted 100 acres near the Parramatta River and within 3 years all the land was cultivated and over 2000 barrels of wheat stored. As a reward they were granted an extra 100 acres in Parramatta. Here they built the beautiful Elizabeth Farm, still Australia's oldest intact building.

In 1809 Macarthur had to leave for England after the furore of the Rum Rebellion. He did not return for 8 years. During this long period Elizabeth had to run the farm alone. She proved to be an excellent farm manager with an instinctive flair for business. She was responsible for the merino flocks, their crops, and the overseeing of all the servants, shepherds and convict labourers. She visited the estates regularly on horse, often alone.

Under Elizabeth's supervision the merinos increased and improved. Governer Macquarie was so impressed he gave her a further 600 acres. Her husband returned but was increasingly mentally disturbed. Eventually in 1832 he was pronounced to be a lunatic and unfit for office. Despite his difficult and often violent nature, Elizabeth remained devoted to him until his death. She died 16 years after him. Unlike many other Australian women pioneers, she never felt the need to return to England as she saw Australia as her home.

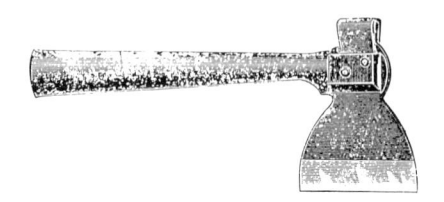

GEORGIANA MOLLOY

The genteel and well educated Georgiana Kennedy was born in 1803 near Carlisle, England. At 24 she married the handsome Captain John Molloy.

The Molloys sailed to the Swan River colony in 1830 and pitched a tent in Fremantle. They found all the best sites along the Swan had already been taken, so they decided to take up land at Augusta, 300 km south of Perth.

While the huge jarrah trees were being cleared, Georgiana lived in a leaking canvas tent with an umbrella above her bed to protect her from the rain. Her first child was born here but soon died. Georgiana was devastated. Eventually the family was living in a small house near the river. They planted their first crops but they were ruined by rust. Georgiana soaked the next crop in salt water before sowing and they fared much better.

Georgiana was lonely and homesick and not very strong. Molloy was often away and she had to face emergencies alone. Once thirty natives came to steal their crop but Georgiana managed to stand up to them even though they shook their spears and one held a broken bottle to her face.

Georgiana had a passion for flowers and planted a beautiful garden of wildflowers, fig trees, vines and peach trees. She became an expert in Western Australian wildflowers.

The Molloys moved to the Vasse district but Georgiana found it hard to leave her garden. However, at her new home, Fair Lawn, she created another delightful garden which became famous throughout the colony.

After the birth of a daughter in 1840 her health was seriously affected and she was confined to bed until she died in 1843.

MARY PENFOLD

Mary arrived in South Australia with her husband, Dr Christopher Rawson Penfold, and their daughter in 1844.

Mary's family brought with them precious vine cuttings from the Rhone area of France. They purchased the 500 acre estate of Magill, a lush and beautiful place in the foothills of the Mount Lofty ranges, 4 km east of Adelaide. Their house was called Grange Cottage.

Mary took up the job of farm manager, while her husband was involved in building up his doctor's practice. Surgery was held in their dining room. Mary helped with the practice as well as overseeing the servants and her daughter's education. However, wine making was Mary's interest and the Magill estate prospered.

By the end of the 1860s Penfolds wines was a flourishing business, Mary managing the business almost single-handedly. At first the wine was used for their own purposes, however, they began to sell and exhibit their wine in Adelaide and won many prizes. Mary found a marketing outlet in Victoria and the business started booming.

In 1870 Christopher died. Mary continued her work on the estate and in 1874 the *Adelaide Register* cited the Penfold vineyards as a fine example of good management.

She was progressive and welcomed technological advancements. By 1891, Penfolds was producing over one-third of all wine in South Australia and selling in all states.

Mary died in Melbourne in 1896.

Leaves from a March Notebook

I like this autumn weather, for it feels like England. Yesterday was still and cold with that dull grey sky we so often have at home in the fall of the year, and today it is pouring with rain, like a genuine English November day. Amy rejoices in the cool weather, and I was tired of the perpetual glare of sunshine. Fine days here bring me no pleasure as they do in England: they are too hot and too numerous, and besides, you cannot enjoy them by taking nice walks – there are no walks to take. [1855]

David Adams, (ed.),
The Letters of Rachel Henning, 1969

AUTUMN

Autumn for the young is the most heady period of the year – March until June...

In Australia there is no fall, except for the imported deciduous trees that are shaken and bowed and emptied of their leaves by strong winds. Our eucalypts drop their dead and rattling foliage and their bark all the time though as a general cleaning up after the summer, a preparation for the partial withdrawal of winter, the rest for soil and plant. An added vigour in the air, a scenting of the future.

Maie Casey, *An Australian Story 1837-1907*, 1962

February ✒ March

MONDAY 26

TUESDAY 27

Shrove Tuesday
1960 Betty Cuthbert ran the 60 m dash in 7.2 seconds

WEDNESDAY 28

Ash Wednesday
1895 b. actress, Louise Lovely
1949 *Blue Hills*, the radio serial, began on ABC radio
1973 Voting age for Federal elections lowered to 18

THURSDAY 1

St David's Day
First day of autumn
Adelaide Festival begins

FRIDAY 2

Moomba Festival begins in Vic.

SATURDAY 3

1819 b. Mercy Sister Ellen Whitty (Mother Vincent)

SUNDAY 4

First quarter of the moon 12.05 pm EST
First Sunday in Lent
Daylight saving ends in SA and NSW
1985 Neighbourhood Watch scheme officially introduced in NSW

		March				
M	T	W	T	F	S	S
			1	2	3	4
5	6	7	8	9	10	11
12	13	14	15	16	17	18
19	20	21	22	23	24	25
26	27	28	29	30	31	

SOME CHARMING EVENING DRESSES

The evening dress of the hour is most alluring. There are a hundred and one dainty little touches which add to its attraction, and the artistic blending of three or four different fabrics and colours makes an ensemble which is delightful. Ideas have been largely borrowed from the East of recent years, and the wide kimona bodice and sleeve now reign supreme. Again inspiration has been drawn from Turkey, for the little hoop tunics certainly owe their origin to that country. These can hardly be said to be really becoming, but they are sufficiently quaint to charm, especially if worn by the right woman, the slender figure once more scoring all along the line. Dame Fashion still clings to the softly-draped underskirt of satin charmeuse, and this forms the foundation to all sorts of diaphanous materials in the way of chiffon, ninon, and crepe de Chine. Each has its own particular charm, for each can be made so easily into the draperies of the moment.

Sydney Mail, June 1914

. . .

OUR SOCIAL EVENING PACKET CONTAINS:

One box containing a White Silk Handkerchief, beautifully embroidered in pretty pale colours; a Pair of White Kid Evening Gloves, 4 buttons, (any size), and a lovely Hair Ornament, together with pretty Chillon Bow and a pretty Pocket Fan and a packet of Violet Powder.

The whole sent post free for 3/-

The Dawn, March 1895

March

MONDAY 5

Labour Day, WA
Trades & Labour Day, ACT
Eight Hours Day, Tas.

TUESDAY 6

1788 First settlement of Norfolk Island

WEDNESDAY 7

1893 b. Helen Louise Gilliar, first woman to compete in the motorcycle reliability trial

THURSDAY 8

International Women's Day
1828 First stamps released in Australia
1910 Mitchell Library in Sydney opened

FRIDAY 9

1836 In support of the Temperance Movement, John Tarvell ordered 600 gallons of rum to be emptied into Sydney Cove
1870 d. cultivator of the Granny Smith apple, Maria Ann Smith

SATURDAY 10

Festival of Perth ends
1881 b. Queen of the Underworld, Kathleen Leigh
1931 Apex Australia formed

SUNDAY 11

Full moon 8.58 pm EST
1835 d. Elizabeth Macquarie
1917 b. writer, Nancy Cato, author of *All the Rivers Run*
1961 Melbourne's Monash University officially opened

M	T	W	T	F	S	S
		1	2	3	4	
5	6	7	8	9	10	11
12	13	14	15	16	17	18
19	20	21	22	23	24	25
26	27	28	29	30	31	

March

Not of Good Character
SOME OF AUSTRALIA'S INFAMOUS WOMEN

As well as Australia's noble dames, we also have our black sheep – infamous women bushrangers, gangsters and murderers, who, like it or not, take their place alongside their more famous male counterparts, as part of our history.

The Cheaters

A DIFFERENT TYPE OF PERSON

The crime queens of Sydney, Tilly Devine and Kate Leigh, were well known for their verbal brawls. Kate Leigh was the sly grog queen of Sydney, while Tilly ran more than twenty brothels. These two women were dominant figures of the Sydney underworld in the 1930s and 1940s. Kate Leigh, who had more than one hundred convictions, despised Tilly. 'How dare you mention my name in the same breath as that woman!', she fumed. 'I am a different type of person and I refuse to even listen to her name.'

Tilly replied, 'I might drink and swear and have a run in with the police now and then, but I don't take dope and no-one can say I have ruined young girls like Kate'.

In truth, neither woman could be said to be of good character. Tilly was married to the notorious 'Big Jim' Devine, who shot dead 'Gunman' Gaffney on their front doorstep, and then shot an innocent taxi driver who arrived with other passengers. Tilly herself was charged with shooting the criminal Eric Parsons with intent to murder. When he recovered he evidently forgave her, because he eventually married her. Kate Leigh shot the notorious Snowy Prendergast, but always maintained she was 'not proud of it' and prayed each night for God to rest his soul.

When Tilly Devine went to England to see

the Coronation in 1953, she took twelve diamond rings, two diamond bracelets, a diamond brooch, a diamond watch and diamond earrings. However, when she died in 1970, she was virtually broke. Kate Leigh also found that crime didn't pay. The Tax Commissioner hit her with an enormous bill for back tax. This, combined with the end of six o'clock closing in 1955, meant the end of her sly grog empire. When she died in 1964, there was little to show for her life of crime.

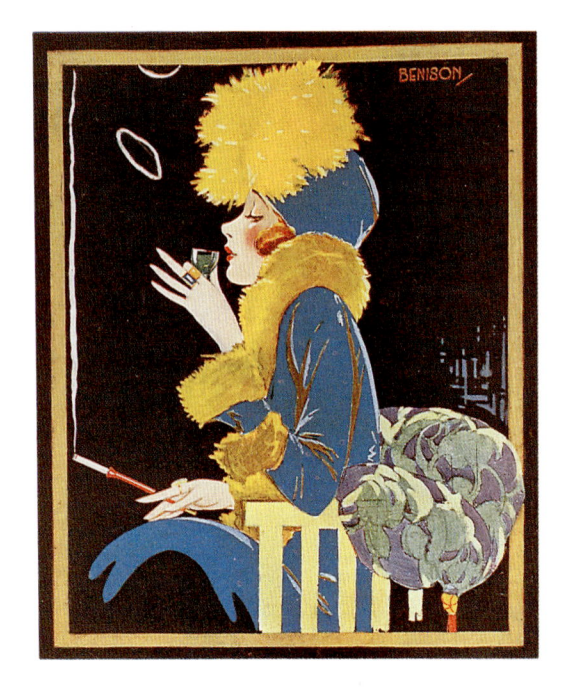

JAZZ BABY

Dark haired, big grey eyes and beautiful legs. That was Ida Pender, wife of the notorious Melbourne crime boss of the 1920s, 'Squizzy' Taylor. Ida, who was known as a wild dresser and an even wilder dancer, met Taylor at the St Kilda Palais de Danse. They also frequented the Jazz Palais, where she acquired the nickname 'Jazz Baby'.

During her marriage to Squizzy, Ida acquired better taste in clothes, took elocution lessons and began to pass herself off as a clergyman's daughter, educated at the best Melbourne private school. She also acquired a criminal record. However, after Squizzy died in 1924, Ida led a quiet suburban life with her daughter Gloria – although she continued to frequent the St Kilda Palais.

From the Police Gazette 6/3/1922: Pender, Ida, is charged on warrant with feloniously breaking and entering the shop of Rita Moore, 183 Glenhuntley Rd, Elsternwick, with intent to steal and did steal a georgette frock; 5 sponge cloth frocks; a number of blouses; and other articles valued at £221, at Elsternwick.

Description: 16½ years, looks older, 5'4", medium build, attractive appearance, brown hair (bobbed), shapely legs, dressed in a reddish brown coat and skirt with suede lapels, blocked felt hat, long veil, fashionably dressed. Fond of jazzing and skating. Is an associate of 'Squizzy' Taylor.

LIME AND LEMON

If women only realised the value of limes and lemons as blood purifiers there would be fewer skin troubles grumbled about. Instead of tea several times a day a few glasses of lime or lemon juice and water would keep the complexion fresh and clear.

Helen's Weekly, November 1927

AN INTERESTING AID TO BEAUTY

Never have women sought so intensely to attract. At one time almost the only weapon in their armoury was clothes. Nowadays clothes are just one of many lures to make a woman charming. Beauty culture is of far greater importance. The face, the eyes, the hair, the figure, the hands, the nails, all come in for intensive treatment in the campaign of attraction that is waged with increasing fervour by modern women. To pick up any magazine dealing with women's interests is to be impressed with the vast number of aids to beauty that are described in the advertising pages. Even an advertisement for chewing gum bases it appeal on its alleged beautifying properties. 'Chewing brings charm to the face by overcoming that set look about the mouth and lips that is so unbecoming' we are told by the chewing gum proprietors.

The Home, February 1932

March

MONDAY 12
Passion Sunday
Labour Day, Vic.
Moomba Festival ends in Vic.
1912 b. writer, Kylie Tennant, author of *Ride on Stranger*

TUESDAY 13

1894 b. medical practitioner, Lady Phyllis Cilento

WEDNESDAY 14

1762 b. convict, pioneer and midwife, Margaret Catchpole

THURSDAY 15
Beware the Ides of March!
1937 d. writer, Catherine Martin, author of *An Australian Girl*
1983 Rosemary Foot was voted Deputy Leader of the NSW Parliament Liberal Party

FRIDAY 16

1873 b. hospital matron, Jane Bell
1897 b. writer, Flora Eldershaw, who wrote under the pseudonym of M. Barnard Eldershaw together with Marjorie Barnard

SATURDAY 17
St Patrick's Day
1871 Alice Springs discovered and named after wife of SA Postmaster General, Alice Todd
1884 b. Aboriginal rights activist, Olive Pink

SUNDAY 18

Adelaide Festival ends
Daylight saving ends in Vic.

		March				
M	T	W	T	F	S	S
			1	2	3	4
5	6	7	8	9	10	11
12	13	14	15	16	17	18
19	20	21	22	23	24	25
26	27	28	29	30	31	

The Aries Birthday
21 MARCH – 20 APRIL

The symbol for the sign Aries is the Ram. Aries rules the head and face. Aries corresponds to the first house in the horoscope, which stands for the personal self. You can usually pick an Aries man or woman or child from one or more of the following points: Bushy eyebrows, and hair that grows off the temples at each side in a little point somewhat resembling the two horns of a Ram. A mark, a mole, a scar, or patch on the head or face, usually dated from birth. Complaints are headaches and insomnia, due to an over-active brain and a tendency to overwork, mentally and physically. The cure is rest and sleep in a dark room.

The Aries typical word in conversations is 'I'. The motto seems to be action! attack!

Aspro Year Book, 1936

SKYBORNE OVER WATER

The first really exciting thing to happen to Sydney in my day was the building of the Harbour Bridge. It was an awakening and an eye-opener. We watched the arch take shape and wondered if its designers and builders could possibly have planned it so true that the halves of the span would meet exactly in the middle. Unforgettable was the marvel and beauty of it when it did. That stupendous arch was as beautiful and magical as a rainbow or cobweb, and likewise of short duration. Once tied to its roadway, it achieved a different kind of splendour, especially at night, but I am grateful that I saw it 50 years ago, when pylons unfinished, it seemed skyborne over the water.

Helen Rutledge, *My Grandfather's House*, 1986

March

MONDAY 19

Canberra Day
1856 Voting by secret ballot became law in Vic., first such system adopted anywhere in the world
1932 Sydney Harbour Bridge opened

TUESDAY 20

Last quarter of the moon 12.30 am EST
1946 d. writer, Henry Handel Richardson (Ethel Florence Lindesay Richardson), author of *The Getting of Wisdom*

WEDNESDAY 21

Autumn equinox 7.19 am EST
1857 b. pioneer of women's trade union movement, Alice Henry
1887 b. artist, Clarice Beckett
1984 d. journalist, Molly Dye

THURSDAY 22

1842 d. pastoralist, Jemima Jenkins

FRIDAY 23

SATURDAY 24

Lady Day
1985 d. radio veteran, Andrea (Dorothy) Jenner, aged 95

SUNDAY 25

1877 d. philanthropist, Caroline Chisholm
1879 d. founder member and first president of the CWA, Grace Munro

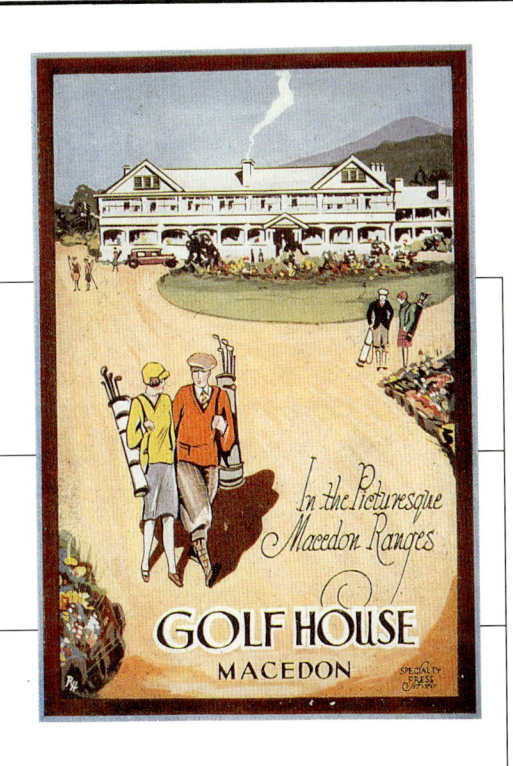

	March					
M	T	W	T	F	S	S
			1	2	3	4
5	6	7	8	9	10	11
12	13	14	15	16	17	18
19	20	21	22	23	24	25
26	27	28	29	30	31	

Women Journalists with the ABC

Life as a journalist can be varied and demanding. Here are some experiences of three women journalists with the ABC.

KATHLEEN VELLACOTT-JONES

In 1948, Kathleen Vellacott-Jones wrote for the ABC's house magazine, *Radio Active*, from Western Australia where she and a group of ABC Radio news reporters had gone for a familiarisation trip. She had to come to grips with names such as Manjimup, Wilgarrup, Kojonup, and so on. 'When we got to Gnowangerup, we tackled the pronunciation by producing something resembling a thoroughly effective gargle' she said. 'Our knowledgeable and co-operative Western Australian typists shook their head and replied, 'No, Angerup.'

There were other problems for a young reporter — not too different from those which occur today. 'One official of a well-known and highly controversial Board demanded why he should give the ABC news, and, just for good measure, added that he didn't think the information wanted was news, anyway. We suggested that the job of a news service was to supply news, and just as he knew all about – well, we'll say peppercorns – we rather figured our business was to know news. The Peppercorn Board chap expressed his indignation by asking why he should pay out chunks of his salary in keeping the ABC going, and for good measure declared that nobody

Kathleen Vellacott-Jones

ever really understood the real function of the Peppercorn organisation. In our best parliamentary manner, modelled on a combination of "Ben" and "Ming" styles, we remarked that "chunks" were chipped off *our* salaries for the Peppercorn Board, and there were people who didn't understand OUR organisation, or try to. Well, we parted the best of friends with our news story in the bag...'

By 1949, Kathleen was working in Papua New Guinea where she found that even the environment offered challenges. 'The centipede season has opened at Port Moresby, and already a major strike has been chalked up. Late one Saturday night an energetic six-inch centipede stretched its hundred legs and decided on a little exploratory work. By the wee sma' hours of the morning its travels had taken it to the recumbent form of the ABC's journalist snoring peacefully under a non-centipede proof net. A hot-needle-like jab in the region of the ribs flashed the alarm signal to the journalistic brain cells, and the battle was on…In the hide-and-seek game which followed all the honors went to the centipede which got in another couple of bites.'

❦ ❦ ❦

MARGARET CLARKE

Although Margaret Clarke contracted polio at the age of seven 'and was never regarded as strong afterwards though I regard myself as perfectly fit', it never diminished her energy for travelling and writing. Even as an undergraduate at Melbourne University, Margaret wrote for commercial magazines and newspapers and when she went to London she continued to write for Melbourne newspapers. She spent some time in New Zealand during World War II as a sub-editor for the *New Zealand Herald*. 'They tried me out as a cable sub when all the men were going to the war and found I could do the job,' she said. 'I had very good training there – it was the premier paper of New Zealand.'

Back in Australia, Margaret worked for the *Sydney Morning Herald* as a sub-editor in the Macquarie Newsroom from which news was broadcast through 2GB, later joining the ABC as a sub-editor on the *ABC Weekly* in 1951.

Margaret remained with the ABC until her retirement in 1976, moving from the *ABC Weekly* to *TV Times* and then to the *ABC Radio Guide*. A writer as well as sub-editor, she continues to contribute in retirement to the ABC's *24 Hours*, usually writing about two of her favourite subjects, books and music.

DIANE WILLMAN

Diane Willman, whose great-grandfather, William Coates Willman, was an executive on the *Sydney Morning Herald* and the *Sydney Mail*, decided at the age of 12 that she would be a journalist, and grew up to become the ABC's correspondent in Lebanon during the civil war of the 1970s.

After a stint as a cadet journalist on a Sydney daily paper she went into radio journalism and became a roving correspondent for the ABC. She went to New Guinea, Burma and India, before marrying a Palestinian and settling in Beirut as a freelance journalist and the ABC's main contact in the Middle East.

The easy-going lifestyle she loved was shattered by the outbreak of the civil war, and Diane's calm voice, often backed by gunfire, was a dramatic link with the conflict in Beirut for listeners to the ABC's programs, 'AM' and 'PM'. Although the family had to live almost permanently in an underground basement and she often had to wrap her small son in a quilt and shield him with her body, Diane never thought of leaving. 'Really, it's too good a story to miss,' she said, 'any journalist would understand.'

Leaves from an April Notebook

It is a lovely luxurious morning, cloudy and gently-falling showers, the beauteous and gigantic Peppermint trees in front of where I write drooping their graceful form. My windows, or rather calico blinds...down, my doors open, the children playing in the verandah, the songsters of the wood chanting it so merrily. I could not refrain from putting some seed in, and just before I sat down, put in some Mignonette, just sent for winter flowering, and some Lilac and Nasturtium seed.

Georgiana Molloy, 1841

CURIOSITIES

Wanted–

Butter from the cream of a joke.
A bucket from 'All Well'.
Eggs from a nest of thieves.
Rockers from the 'Cradle of Liberty'.
A sketch from a politician's views.
A buckle to fasten a laughing stock.
A feather from the wing of a flying report.
The saucer belonging to the cup of sorrow.
A portion of the yeast used in raising the wind.
The brush used in painting 'the sign of the times'.
A fence made from the railings of a scolding wife.
The pencil with which Britannia ruled the waves.
The strop which is used to sharpen the water's edge.

The Dawn, March 1895

March *April*

MONDAY 26

1984 Introduction of the $100 note

TUESDAY 27

New moon 5.48 am EST
1797 Australia's first animal pound established at Sydney Cove
1851 b. feminist author, Rosa Praed

WEDNESDAY 28

1791 d. Mary Bryant, convict who escaped from the colony in an open boat, was recaptured and later became the first convict to return to England
1877 First shearing machine patented

THURSDAY 29

1860 b. nurse, Nellie Gould
1901 First Federal elections

FRIDAY 30

1984 Sally-Anne Atkinson elected Mayor of Brisbane

SATURDAY 31

1908 Female suffrage introduced in Vic.

SUNDAY 1

April Fool's Day
1899 b. physician and scientist, Dame Jean MacNamara

			March			
M	T	W	T	F	S	S
				1	2	3	4
5	6	7	8	9	10	11
12	13	14	15	16	17	18
19	20	21	22	23	24	25
26	27	28	29	30	31	

April

LOVE'S SAFETY VALVE

What would modern woman be without the movies? The answer is easy – she would be a nervous wreck; and so would her husband. Few modern men realise the noble work that is being done by that handful of Perfect Lovers whose stern yet passionate profiles decorate all the most important hoardings of our cities. And it is being done for *them* – yes, for them! Like atheists babbling against the Providence that sustains them, the man of to-day sneers at the 'side-levers' of the incomparable ones, makes jests at the expense of their pure, clear-cut features and the natural marcel wave that glorifies their proud heads. Ah, little does he guess how much the Valentinos have done to keep the gas-fires burning undimmed on his domestic hearth!

Emancipated woman has discovered herself capable of a Great Love (the 'orange-grove and marble courtyard' variety), but scarcely any husband is a Great Lover. (When he is it usually finishes up with a long queue waiting to get into the Divorce Court to hear the evidence.) It remains for the incomparable ones of the screen to offer romance to panting modern hearts – in two-and-a-half-hour doses – and send them home happy...

And until our souls are as wide-awake as our imaginations the inimitable Rudolphs will continue to be Love's Safety Valve.

Dulcie Deamer, *Australian Woman's Mirror*, November 1926

MONDAY 2

First quarter of the moon 8.24 pm EST
1936 b. politician, Rosemary Foot
1978 d. actress and muscial comedy star, Gloria Dawn
1985 d. theatrical producer, Doris Fitton

TUESDAY 3

1881 Australia's first census totalled the country's white population at 2.25 million
1925 May Holman became first woman Labor MP in WA

WEDNESDAY 4

1879 b. physician and child care authority, Margaret Harper
1984 Janice Crosio became first woman cabinet minister in NSW

THURSDAY 5

1878 b. missionary, Retta Long
1932 Champion horse Phar Lap died of colic from suspected poisoning in California

FRIDAY 6

Royal Easter Show begins in Sydney
1895 Words and music of 'Waltzing Matilda' first sung in public at the North Gregory Hotel, Winton, Qld.

SATURDAY 7

1845 b. feminist and temperance advocate, Margaret McLean
1969 First Weight Watchers International meeting held in Sydney

SUNDAY 8

Palm Sunday
1905 Muriel Chase (Aunt Mary) began Silver Chain Appeal for sick children in WA
1958 d. writer, Ethel Turner, author of *Seven Little Australians*

		April				
M	T	W	T	F	S	S
30						1
2	3	4	5	6	7	8
9	10	11	12	13	14	15
16	17	18	19	20	21	22
23	24	25	26	27	28	29

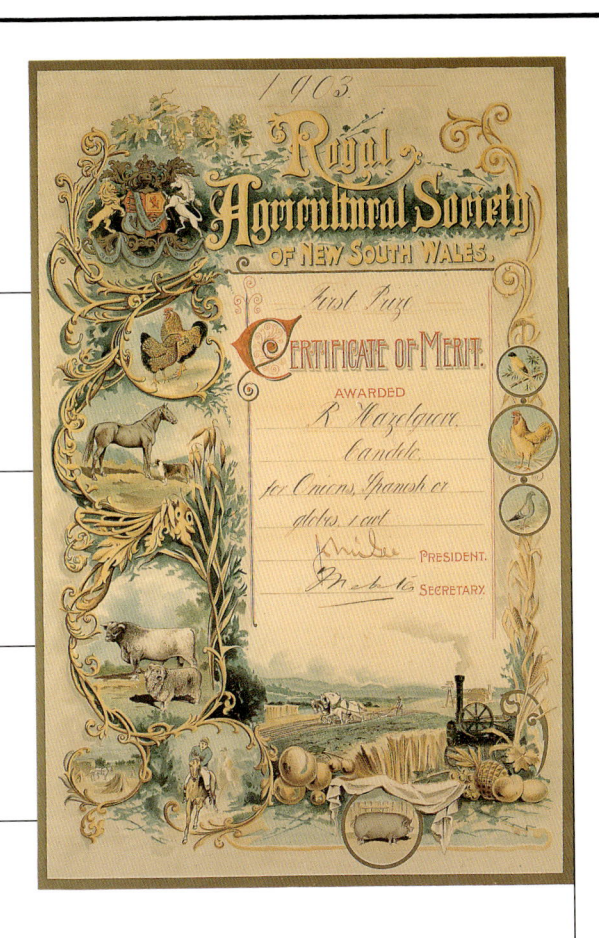

YOUNG HOUSEKEEPERS SHOULD KNOW

That soda will clean tarnished tin.
That vinegar and salt will clean copper.
That baking soda put on a burn will take out the heat.
That a heated knife will cut hot bread without making it heavy.
That toilet sets and all chamber articles should be cleaned in cold water.
That a small paint brush should be used in cracks and crevices while dusting a room.
That diseases often lurk in a dirty dishcloth, a greasy sink, an unclean tea-kettle, and a poorly ventilated oven.
That flannels should be washed in soap-suds, and rinsed in hot water containing soap enough to soften it a little.
That silver should be washed with a chamois leather saturated with soap each time after use, thus avoiding a general cleaning.
That preserving jars should be stood on their heads for at least an hour after sealing when the liquor will escape if the jar contains air.

The Dawn, January 1895

April

MONDAY 9

1902 British citizens in Australia received full voting rights for Federal Parliament
1987 d. writer, Mary Edgeworth David

TUESDAY 10

Full moon 1.18 pm EST
1851 b. actress, Maggie Moore
1946 b. composer, Anne Boyd

WEDNESDAY 11

1955 d. welfare worker and social reformer, Jeanne Young
1984 'Advance Australia Fair' adopted as National Anthem

THURSDAY 12

Maundy Thursday
1905 d. bushranger, Mary Ann Baker

FRIDAY 13

Good Friday
1869 b. feminist and suffragette, Vida Goldstein
1892 b. singer, Gladys Moncrieff
1969 Last tram ran in Brisbane

SATURDAY 14

Easter Saturday
1933 Lores Bonney took off from Darwin on her record-breaking flight to London

SUNDAY 15

Easter Sunday

		April				
M	T	W	T	F	S	S
30						1
2	3	4	5	6	7	8
9	10	11	12	13	14	15
16	17	18	19	20	21	22
23	24	25	26	27	28	29

The Australian Home

Although Australia's architecture has always borrowed much from European traditions, our homes have a style that is recognisable even in the homes of our first settlers.

WALLPAPER PANELLING
—the newest, most attractive decoration for walls

EVEN in the smallest rooms, wallpaper panelling is an improvement on other methods of wall decoration. It is surprisingly inexpensive and easily carried out. There is nothing more in keeping with modern furnishings—nothing brighter or more attractive in effect.

WASHABLE, NON-FADING

Sanitas Wall Covering can be wiped clean and fresh with a damp cloth. No risk of soiled walls—even in kitchens. No marks from soot, smoke or passing hands of children or adults. Call and see the new patterns or write for samples.

Small rooms look best panelled in light tinted wallpaper. Soft, light yellow, cream or buff tones are most suitable. For larger rooms select figured panels in stronger colours.

Before deciding to have painted walls—before buying any wallpaper—inspect the panels displayed in our showroom. See exactly the fine effects that are produced. If unable to call, write for wallpaper samples, stating favourite colours.

JAMES SANDY & CO. LIMITED
326-8 GEORGE STREET, SYDNEY 'Phone BW 1941 123 SCOTT STREET, NEWCASTLE

THE LATEST DESIGN

Ned and Edith's bathroom, which was not 'ensuite', was unlike any other bathroom I have seen. It had a very deep bath with a flat bottom, almost as cold and hard to heat as marble. It was surrounded with pine panelling and one end was enclosed for an overhead shower – a roof with holes in it. On three sides were needle sprays and a swinging half door on the fourth side. Let into the panelling, were controls to pull and push to let the water in and out through ornamental gratings. There were no taps, spouts or plugs. We were not allowed to use the sprays, though we wanted to be 'needled', as the 'controls' had lost all power to regulate the water temperature, if they ever did. I doubt if they were ever used because the water pressure on Bellevue Hill, before its water tower was built, was very weak.

The bath came from J. Finch, 9 Buckingham Street, Strand, London. It was shipped on 1 December 1883. It was described on the invoice as 'Porcelain Bath in One Piece, designed by his late Royal Highness, the Prince Consort'. It won medals in 1850 and 1851 in the Great Exhibition and 1861 in the International Exhibition. Rather dated really. Included without charge were three china perforated plates for the sprays, and the cost was £9.18.8.

Helen Rutledge, *My Grandfather's House*, 1986

A PLEASANT HOUSE

Inside the house was very pleasant. The double drawing-room with the two big arches of the verandah were glazed to north and west with French doors on to the verandah. This room had a particularly pretty Wunderlich plaster ceiling with Australian motifs of waratahs, wattle and lyrebirds' tails. The dining-room had a more restrained pattern of geometric interlacing curves...

The most handsome feature of the house was the effective use of cedar. Handsome panelled doors had wide architraves. The staircase was of real distinction, and perhaps an unwarranted extravagance. It went round three sides of the hall and the upstairs landing completed the fourth side.

It was a house to be run by three live-in maids and had quarters built for them. There were only four large bedrooms in front, one too few for a family of five as no dressing room had been attached to my mother's room.

Helen Rutledge, *My Grandfather's House*, 1986

WHAT AN ATROCITY!

An atrocious feature in many unpretentious Australian homes is the ready-made mantelpiece. Nothing satisfactory can be done with a room – no matter how pleasing it may be otherwise – suffering from one of these vulgarities, in which a surprising amount of contorted wood, indescribable brackets, treacly varnish and cheap mirror is included at a cost of a few pounds, to the despair of every conscientious architect and designer ... Another atrocity in many homes is constituted by the gas and electric fittings. Many of those imported into this country, excepting the simplest and purely utilitarian forms, seem to indicate that Australia is the dumping ground for much rubbish from America and Europe. At any rate, few of the good designs used even in ordinary middle-class houses, especially in America, are to be seen locally. It would be much more satisfactory if Australia manufactured for her own supply in good models.

Sydney Mail, June 1914

The Taurus Birthday
20 APRIL – 20 MAY

The symbol for the sign Taurus is a Bull, and Taurus rules the throat and palate. Taurus corresponds to the second house of the horoscope, and stands for money and income. You can usually pick a Taurus person by his large dark eyes, wide nostrils, broad shoulders, thick neck, and dusky colouring. But be prepared for some slender, blue-eyed specimens, if other planets predominate at birth. Taurus people often stamp and kick the ground with their feet whilst standing waiting, much like a bull pawing the earth.

Sane, solid, and steady by nature, they resist all attempt to bustle or change them! Taurus folk are strong, vital people, often with good singing voices, but sometimes with a tendency to throat afflictions. They like nice things to eat, but they must regulate their meals for health's sake.

Their great word in conversation is 'Wait!' their motto 'Stability'.

You won't mind living in timbered country, in houses surrounded by trees, or in low rooms, and caves and cellars do not frighten you.

Money should roll to you.

Aspro Year Book, 1936

April

MONDAY 16

Easter Monday
1894 b. opera singer, Florence Austral
1910 University of Queensland founded

TUESDAY 17

Easter Tuesday, Vic.
Bank holiday, Tas.
Royal Easter Show ends in Sydney
1941 Women's Royal Australian Naval Service (WRANS) formed

WEDNESDAY 18

Last quarter of the moon 5.02 pm EST
1951 d. anthropologist, Daisy Bates
1966 First National Service troops left for Vietnam

THURSDAY 19

1876 b. politician, Elizabeth Couchman
1941 Ola Cohn's Pioneer Women's Memorial unveiled in Adelaide

FRIDAY 20

1770 James Cook first sighted south-east Australia
1938 b. athlete, Betty Cuthbert

SATURDAY 21

1856 First railway in Australia opened, Adelaide to Port Adelaide
1925 d. feminist and social reformer, Rose Scott
1926 b. Queen Elizabeth II

SUNDAY 22

Low Sunday
Yom Hasho'ah (Holocaust Remembrance Day)
1891 NSW Women's Suffrage League first met

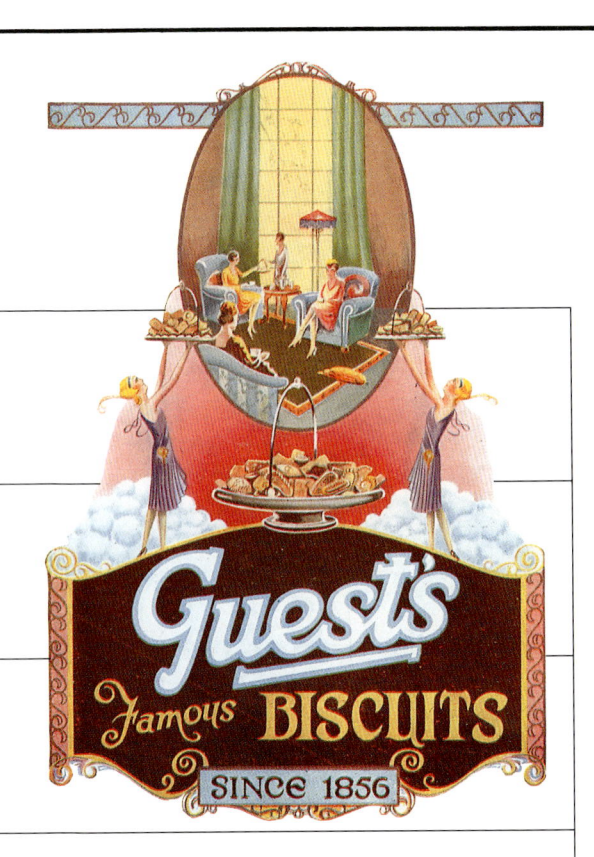

	April					
M	T	W	T	F	S	S
30						1
2	3	4	5	6	7	8
9	10	11	12	13	14	15
16	17	18	19	20	21	22
23	24	25	26	27	28	29

April

RENDEZVOUS

Long before the dawn breaks
With a bird's cry,
I'll be hustling on the wind
Out to where you lie –
Hurrying to our rendezvous
Under the April sky.

I'll step from out the sea again
To the shoulder of the land,
And pass the dead boy where he lies
Prone on the tideless strand,
Treading lightly lest I move
His fingers in the sand.

Do you remember how you stopped
After the sudden climb,
Sniffing the air as one who comes
On a holy thing sublime?
I'll meet you where the breeze brought
The first scent of thyme.

I'll meet you where we yarned that morn
Under the April sky,
Waiting on our bellies there
For the battle cry.
I'll meet you where I left you there
Lying all awry.
You said, 'We will continue the
Discussion by and by.'

*If I could but remember what
We spoke of you, and I!*

Leon Gellert in *The Home*, April 1928

MONDAY 23

St George's Day
1858 b. feminist and teacher, Bella Lavender
1908 b. artist, Margo Lewers

TUESDAY 24

1876 b. nurse and army matron, Ethel Gray

WEDNESDAY 25

New moon 2.27 pm EST
Anzac Day
1809 Australia's first post office opened in Sydney
1871 NSW Academy of Art founded

THURSDAY 26

St Mark's Day
1892 b. artist, Grace Cossington-Smith
1922 b. founder of the Australian Ballet School, Dame Catherine Scott

FRIDAY 27

1789 Mutiny on the *Bounty*

SATURDAY 28

1882 b. feminist, Mildred Muscio
1891 Queen Victoria Museum and Art Gallery opened in Launceston, Ta

SUNDAY 29

1770 Captain Cook landed at Botany Bay
1826 b. writer of letters, Rachel Henning
1875 b. artist, Margaret Preston
1988 Australian Stockman's Hall of Fame opened in Longreach, Qld

		April				
M	T	W	T	F	S	S
30						1
2	3	4	5	6	7	8
9	10	11	12	13	14	15
16	17	18	19	20	21	22
23	24	25	26	27	28	29

Leaves from a May Notebook

I wish I could give you the least idea of the beauty of the scenery here. It was a lovely morning, and we wound along one side of the hill with a deep ravine on our right, and, on the other side of the ravine, a wall of rock that seemed to rise up to the sky with trees growing out of every crevice and the sun shining on the top, while all below was in black shade. I had forgotten how magnificent those Blue Mountains were. We travelled among them all day, over such roads as I never saw before. We had a capital driver, fearless and yet careful, and he took us safe over rocks and ruts and deep holes and fallen trees.

Once we certainly took off the head of a sapling and then got aground on the stump, but the united exertions of the gentlemen lifted the coach off and we got under way again…

We went down Mount Victoria just at sunrise, and some of the views were lovely.

You looked down on seas of forest and fold after fold of mountains covered with wood. I should have enjoyed it more perhaps if I had been walking, instead of in a loaded coach coming down a steep hill over the worst road you can imagine, and with a precipice rising up on the left and another on the right going sheer down I don't know how many hundred feet, and no parapet, so that a shying horse, or a wheel coming off, or an overturn, would have sent us all into another world most likely.

[1861]

David Adams (ed.), *The Letters of Rachel Henning*, 1969

April / May

MONDAY 30
1838 Botanical Gardens in Sydney first opened
1983 d. dancer, Kathleen Gornam

TUESDAY 1
1849 Transportation of convicts to WA began
1856 b. writer, Katie Langloh Parker, author of *Australian Legendary Tales*

WEDNESDAY 2
First quarter of the moon 6.18 am EST
Birthday of Lord Buddha
1888 b. neuro-anatomist, Una Lucy Fielding
1970 d. children's writer, Nan Chauncey, author of *They Found a Cave*

THURSDAY 3
Sts Philip and James' Day
1896 Agricultural Society of NSW held first show in Sydney

FRIDAY 4

SATURDAY 5
1875 b. policewoman and welfare worker, Kate Cocks

SUNDAY 6
1915 Sydney Conservatorium of Music officially opened

	M	T	W	T	F	S	S
May		1	2	3	4	5	6
	7	8	9	10	11	12	13
	14	15	16	17	18	19	20
	21	22	23	24	25	26	27
	28	29	30	31			

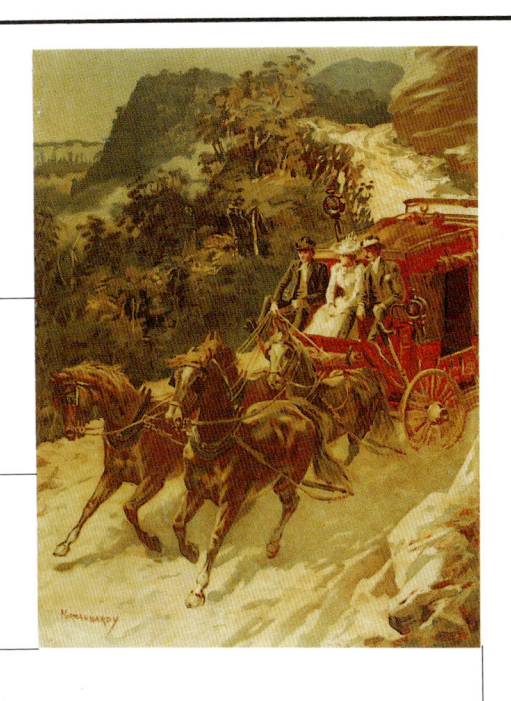

Mother's Day

GRANDMA'S COMING!

Word would fly around the place: 'Grandma's coming, Grandma's coming,' so we'd all go into a real tear. Mother knew she'd be criticized if Grandma saw the place as it was, so there'd be a mad rush for the broom and the tidy-up. We'd all try to clean up before Grandma got from the bottom of the track to the top...

Grandma would pull up at the gate and wait for the boys to run down and open it for her.

One day they were churning the butter when she arrived and they were so excited they knocked the churn over and spilt all the butter.

Grandma always sounded very severe, but she wasn't really – she just had a growly voice.

'Take your hands out of your pockets,' she'd say.

I s'pose she felt entitled since it was she who bought the suits...

When Mother and Aunty were young, Grandma used to stitch all their clothes by hand, even the little frilly white panties, with layers of lace and straight legs, that they wore under their dresses. When sewing machines became fashionable, she refused to believe they were any good so, if she bought ready-made clothes, she would unstitch them and re-stitch them by hand.

Elaine McKenna, *Better than Dancing*, 1987

ENDEARING FEMININE FOIBLES

My mother's robust and businesslike attitude to life was balanced by the most endearing feminine foibles. When she was pleased by her appearance and surveyed the finished work in the mirror before applying a dab of scent behind the ears, she would make the gentle hissing sound one makes when grooming a horse. Possibly there was a subconscious connection in her mind, based on preparedness, through the amount of horse she had groomed. (In that case I was always told that the reason one hissed was to prevent the inhaling of dust from their coats.)

A second habit was that of speaking out of a corner of her mouth when she was saying something she did not want me to hear. I was delighted by this as I knew at once when to listen which I did not usually bother to do.

Maie Casey, *An Australian Story 1837-1907*, 1962

May

FASHION AND THE HOME

The fashion chat to-day is mainly about blouses. These have become such a necessity that they are sufficiently important to be seriously discussed. Some of the latest styles are extremely artistic.

The weather has been so cold lately that the thickest of dresses and cosiest of wraps have been requisitioned to keep out the keen wind; but the collarless neck reigns supreme, and in the house quite bare throats are general. Some well-known London doctors are now arguing that this is a very good thing, as it helps to strengthen the base of the throat and makes for health. Spartan measures are the order of the day. At any rate, the low-cut neck is decidedly comfortable, and any of last year's blouses available have all been altered to bring them up to date.

Sydney Mail, June 1914

CHERRY MOUSSE

One pint of cream, three tablespoonsful of sugar, one-half teaspoonful of vanilla and one cupful of cherry juice. Whip with a Trellis egg-beater, put in a close-covered mould and pack in broken ice and rock salt for two hours. It will turn out like a mould of ice-cream, but when cut will be in little needle-like flakes. It is a delicious dessert.

The Dawn, December 1894

MONDAY 7
May Day, NT
Labour Day, Qld
1908 King Edward VII granted Australian Commonwealth the Coat of Arms featuring the emu and kangaroo

TUESDAY 8
1840 b. property owner, Elizabeth Macarthur-Onslow
1876 d. Truganini, last full-blooded Tas. Aborigine
1928 First Flying Doctor Service began at Cloncurry, Qld

WEDNESDAY 9
1901 First Parliament of the Australian Commonwealth opened
1927 First Parliament House opened in Canberra

THURSDAY 10
Full moon 5.31 am EST

FRIDAY 11
1929 Irene Longman became the first woman to enter Qld Parliament

SATURDAY 12
1777 b. pioneer businesswoman, Mary Reiby
1902 Ada Evans became first Australian woman law graduate
1934 d. founder of St Margaret's Hospital, Mother Abbott (Gertrude Abbott)
1972 Women's Electoral Lobby (WEL) founded

SUNDAY 13
Mother's Day
1787 First Fleet set sail from Portsmouth
1845 b. writer and journalist, Emily Manning
1984 Introduction of the $1 coin

	M	T	W	T	F	S	S
May		1	2	3	4	5	6
	7	8	9	10	11	12	13
	14	15	16	17	18	19	20
	21	22	23	24	25	26	27
	28	29	30	31			

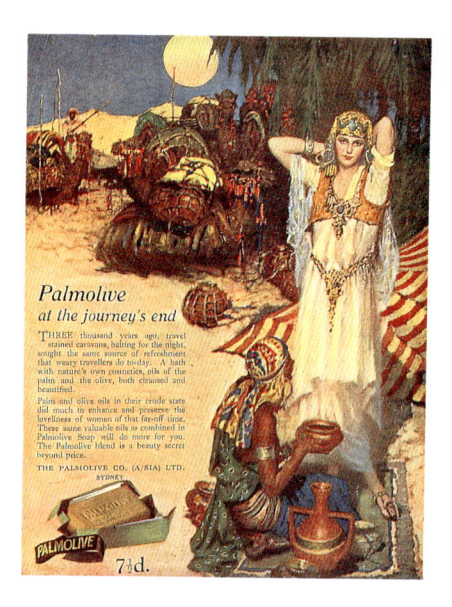

WISHFUL THINKING

Two other acquaintances who stayed with us were Amy and Polly Unwin, two spinsters from Singleton...

Even in late middle age when neither could be called exactly comely, they led a most exciting secret life. I shall never forget the first time I accompanied Miss Amy into town and found myself suddenly pushed into a doorway as three poor lascars off some ship happened to pass. 'Psst!' she hissed. 'White slavers!' She refused to enter Quong Tart's or walk down Campbell Street, where I hoped to find some cumquats to preserve, because as well as being full of opium dens, the street was also full of lascivious orientals bent on deflowering Australian virgins.

'That man has his eye on me,' said Polly, indicating the postman. 'Don't worry,' said Mother soothingly, 'the penalty for rape is death' – a statement which I think showed a certain frivolity of outlook. Even when staying in my husband's home many years later, they noisily locked their bedroom door every night, much to his astonishment.

Eugénie McNeil and Eugénie Crawford, *Ladies Didn't*, 1984

May

MONDAY 14

1855 Royal Mint opened in Sydney

TUESDAY 15

1888 Louisa Lawson first published the women's paper, the *Dawn*
1926 b. politician, Dame Margaret Guilfoyle

WEDNESDAY 16

1868 b. artist, Bessie Gibson
1893 b. portrait painter and official war artist, Esther Bowen

THURSDAY 17

FRIDAY 18

Last quarter of the moon 5.45 am EST
1876 d. Julia Matthews, actress and sweetheart of Robert O'Hara Burke
1890 b. poet, Zora Cross
1905 Qld women voted for the first time in a state election

SATURDAY 19

1861 b. opera singer, Dame Nellie Melba (Helen Porter Armstrong)

SUNDAY 20

1926 b. first woman mayor, Margaret Armitage

		May				
M	T	W	T	F	S	S
	1	2	3	4	5	6
7	8	9	10	11	12	13
14	15	16	17	18	19	20
21	22	23	24	25	26	27
28	29	30	31			

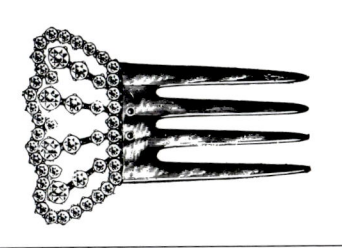

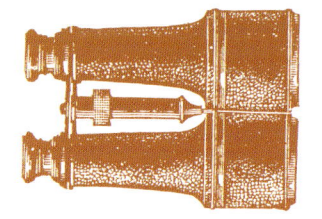

WOMEN RACEHORSE TRAINERS

'Cuna': *Apropos* women racehorse trainers. On the Eastern Goldfields of W.A. it is quite a common sight to see trotters being ridden at work by wives or daughters of owners. About every three months the Trotting Club includes a Ladies Race in the programme and it is easily the most popular event of the evening (they race under electric light). Punters lose cheerfully on this event because they know they get a 'straight go' – pride in their skill keeps these riders above corruption.

Australian Woman's Mirror, October 1926

BILL SMITH

Jockey Bill Smith, born in 1886, arrived in North Queensland with two racehorses. He established himself as a well known identity on country racecourses. He was said to be a small figure, very roughly spoken who swore all the time. He was thought to be very eccentric when he refused to change with the other jockeys. He won many races including the St Leger Quest in 1902, the Jockey Club Derby in 1903, and the Victorian Oaks in 1909-1910. The last four years of Bill Smith's life were spent in Cairns where he lived as a recluse. He died in 1975 and only then was it discovered that Bill Smith was in fact a woman. She was buried under the name of Wilhelmina Smith.

May

MONDAY 21
Adelaide Cup Day
1923 b. playwright, Dorothy Hewett, author of *The Man from Mukinupin*

TUESDAY 22
1802 Matthew Flinders discovered Kangaroo Island off the coast of SA
1932 d. Labor leader, feminist and social worker, Jean Beadle

WEDNESDAY 23
Yom Yerushalayim (Jerusalem Day)
1805 b. early settler and botanist, Georgiana Molloy

THURSDAY 24
New moon 9.47 pm EST
1841 Sydney first lit with gas
1861 National Gallery of Victoria founded
1878 b. writer, Mary Grant Bruce, author of the *Billabong* series

FRIDAY 25
1896 Women voted for the first time in SA
1947 b. actress, Jackie Weaver

SATURDAY 26
1853 Last convict arrived in Hobart
1955 d. Mollie Skinner, co-author with D.H. Lawrence of *The Boy in the B*
1980 High Court of Australia building opened in Canberra

SUNDAY 27
1967 Referendum gave Aboriginal people the vote

		May				
M	T	W	T	F	S	S
	1	2	3	4	5	6
7	8	9	10	11	12	13
14	15	16	17	18	19	20
21	22	23	24	25	26	27
28	29	30	31			

Women Photographers

Australia's history has been short and the camera has seen much of it. Women feature quite early in Australia's photographic history. They have recorded much of our history and, in particular, the domestic history. However, until recently their work has remained unknown or unrecognised. This year, we feature some of Australia's greatest women photographers.

Teacup Ballet, Olive Cotton

OLIVE COTTON

Olive Cotton, born in 1911, was interested in photography from a young age. As a teenager she met and started to work with a family friend, photographer Max Dupain, and they worked together. Olive's first enlarger was home-made and constructed from old tins!

In 1929 Olive and Max joined the Photographic Society of New South Wales and the Sydney Camera Club, where they met leading photographers such as Harold Cazneaux.

Olive graduated from the University of Sydney in 1934 and began work in Max Dupain's studio which was just beginning to have some success. They were regarded as the 'new talent'.

Olive carried out a lot of commercial work. Her first exhibition was with the Photographic Society's exhibition of 1932. She was a great technician and her work displays a magnificent use of light. Two of her best-known photographs, *Teacup Ballet* and *Shasta Daisies*, were shown in London.

In 1938, Olive and Max moved from their Bond Street studio to new larger premises at Clarence Street. They married in 1939 and divorced in 1940, although they continued to work together. When Max enlisted in World War II, Olive ran the Clarence Street studio. The following years, until 1945, were the greatest of her career.

Olive married again and she and her

husband moved to Cowra. She had two children. While in Cowra she took many photographs of children and the landscape. She returned to photography full-time in 1964, opening a studio in Cowra.

The Australian Centre for Photography held a retrospective of Olive Cotton's work in 1985.

MAY AND MINA MOORE

May Moore was born in 1881 and Mina in 1882, in Auckland. As May showed an artistic bent when she was young, she was sent to art school. The two sisters were keen to become photographers, although they had no previous experience at all. They set out to learn the art as fast as they could. They obtained a studio in Wellington and hired two assistants. The studio quickly became established. They used limp mounting boards and photographic paper with a canvas-like finish which gave their work a distinctive look.

In 1910, May travelled to Australia while Mina remained behind in Auckland to run the studio on a professional basis. May was lent a studio in Sydney in the building where the *Bulletin* was published. She soon gained a reputation as a talented artist and shrewd businesswoman.

Mina came to Australia in 1913, establishing a studio in Collins Street, Melbourne. She worked with a journalist taking photographs of people interviewed, including Dame Nellie Melba.

Mina was married in 1916, and after the birth of her daughter, retired from photography. She only undertook one more job – for Shell in 1927 – converting her kitchen into a darkroom for a time.

The *Lone Hand* and *Triad* reproduced many of May and Mina Moore's photographs. May died in 1931 aged 50, and Mina in 1957 aged 75.

Portrait of a woman, May and Mina Moore

BERNICE AGAR

Bernice Agar, born in 1885, was one of Sydney's leading photographers in the 1920s. Her photographic portraits were quite dramatic and imbued the sitters with larger-than-life qualities. Bernice Agar's work featured frequently in the stylish *Home* magazine as she specialised in portraits, often of high society figures. Bernice herself was a glamorous woman, always beautifully dressed. At 44 she married and soon after retired from photography. She lived until she was 91.

Leaves from a June Notebook

And there are other bright memories of Adelaide, notably Adams, a merry soul from Hill and Co.'s stables, who taught present scribe the delights of four-in-hand driving, thereby offering endless facilities for desecrating the virtuous Adelaide Sabbath. To Adams, a vote of thanks! and a thrill of real enthusiasm when I remember those crisp June mornings, the thud of the bloods' hoofs in the frosty stillness, the scent of the fragrant earth – peace in my heart, sunshine abroad, and, for the time, the petty mortifications of my surroundings forgotten. Ah! Those were good days.

Thistle Anderson, *Arcardian Adelaide*, 1905

WINTER

Winter is comparatively mild and never flowerless. Our houses, designed for some other land, some other climate, may face our strongest winds broadside on; trees and their comforting protection are often spurned. For children there is an early retreat into indoor life away from the darkness that falls so swiftly for us, denying the twilight of northern countries.

Maie Casey, *An Australian Story 1837-1907*, 1962

May June

MONDAY 28

Chinese Dragon Boat Festival
1860 b. founder of hospitals, Anne Daly (Mother Mary Berchmans)
1963 d. artist, Margaret Preston

TUESDAY 29

1909 b. Joyce Steele, first woman to enter SA Parliament and to hold a ministerial post
1924 d. caterer, Charlotte Sargent, instigator of Sargent's Pies

WEDNESDAY 30

Shavuot
1918 b. The Reverend Hilda May Abba, first woman to be ordained in Australia

THURSDAY 31

First quarter of the moon 6.11 pm EST
1915 b. poet and conservationist, Judith Wright
1918 b. tennis star, Thelma Long
1926 b. writer and historian, Patsy Adam-Smith

FRIDAY 1

First day of winter
1829 Foundation of WA
1912 Commonwealth Bank opened for business
1937 b. writer, Colleen McCullough, author of *The Thorn Birds*

SATURDAY 2

1916 Goanna Oil trademark registered
1953 Coronation of Queen Elizabeth II
1987 NT Government gave Lindy Chamberlain a pardon following release of the Morling Report

SUNDAY 3

Pentecost
1887 b. army nurse, Rosa Kirkcaldie
1929 b. botanical artist, Betty Conabere

			May			
M	T	W	T	F	S	S
	1	2	3	4	5	6
7	8	9	10	11	12	13
14	15	16	17	18	19	20
21	22	23	24	25	26	27
28	29	30	31			

The Gemini Birthday
21 MAY – 20 JUNE

The symbol for the sign Gemini is a pair of Twins. Gemini rules the hands, arms, collarbones and lungs. Gemini corresponds with the third house in the horoscope, and rules the over-active mind, and also rules travel.

Gemini people needn't worry about taking exercise. Their naturally active minds keep them chasing, but they DO need plenty of sleep, for they are very highly strung.

In appearance, Gemini people are usually long in the arms, and tend to have slender hands, with long fingers, and to be tall and slight in build. But appearance varies, and you can pick them easiest by their habits and little ways!
The Gemini word is 'Why?' the motto 'Investigation.'

Aspro Year Book, 1936

MY NATIVE GIRL

Before thy love this bosom blessed
    And thrilling rapture shed,
No care my thoughtless heart confessed,
    I roamed where fancy led.
But since thy beauty's spell came o'er
    My heart, no longer free,
Each hour enchains it still the more,
    My native girl to thee.

In vain may other beauties smile
    To shake my love sincere;
If absent from thy side the while
    Thy image still is near.
Thy lover's heart wherein it dwells
    Its chosen shrine must be,
Ne'er to be lured by others' spells.
    My native girl from thee. [1844]

The Currency Lass, 1975

June

MONDAY 4

Foundation Day, WA
1851 b. philanthropist, Lady Janet Clarke
1857 b. writer, Barbara Baynton, author of *Bush Studies*
1923 b. writer, Elizabeth Jolley, author of *Mr Scobie's Riddle*

TUESDAY 5

1831 d. 'the Amazon of Van Diemen's Land', Tarereenore
1870 b. Jeannie (Mrs Aeneas) Gunn, author of *We of the Never Never*
1984 Federal Government outlined the Affirmative Action campaign to improve the position of women in the Australian labour force

WEDNESDAY 6

THURSDAY 7

1899 d. feminist, Annette Bear-Crawford
1944 Butter rationing began in Australia

FRIDAY 8

Full moon 9.01 pm EST
1920 b. poet, Gwen Harwood

SATURDAY 9

1887 b. headmistress, Fanny Cohen
1961 d. Jeannie (Mrs Aeneas) Gunn, author of *We of the Never Never*

SUNDAY 10

Trinity Sunday
1835 Australia's first political party, the Patriotic Party, established
1933 The *Australian Women's Weekly* first published

		June				
M	T	W	T	F	S	S
				1	2	3
4	5	6	7	8	9	10
11	12	13	14	15	16	17
18	19	20	21	22	23	24
25	26	27	28	29	30	

LAUNDERING STOCKINGS
General Rules

1. Treat according to the material of which they are made.
2. Do not wash in water in which anything else has been washed.
3. Shake dust from stockings.
4. Wash first on right side, paying particular attention to the soles.
5. Turn and wash on the wrong side.
6. Knead and squeeze until all dirt is removed.
7. Rinse thoroughly.
8. When wringing, pass through wringer toes first, or squeeze water out by rolling up from the foot to the knee.
9. Peg out on wrong side, with the toes about 1 inch over the line.
10. When dry, fold in 3 even parts, the toes being on top, press if necessary.
11. If new stockings are washed before they are worn, they wear better and any loose dye is removed.

Common Sense Laundry Book, 1942

BLOOMERS

Elastic was first used for bloomers which Mrs Bloomer invented for cycling. They were soon worn by everyone, partly for warmth, instead of a flannel petticoat. My own experience with bloomers was that the elastic in the legs was either too tight and you were told not to wriggle or too loose and one leg hung down. We wore so much underwear with our combinations, binders, liberty bodices, flannel petticoats, woollen bloomers and extra vests that no heating was required for our nurseries except in the case of illness. If very cold, I suppose we were buttoned up in overcoats.

Helen Rutledge, *My Grandfather's House*, 1986

June

MONDAY 11

Queen's birthday holiday (all states except WA)

TUESDAY 12

1789 Hawkesbury River, NSW, named by Governor Phillip
1872 Royal Mint in Melbourne opened. It closed in 1966
1887 b. businesswoman, Nell Martyn

WEDNESDAY 13

1778 b. Elizabeth Macquarie
1861 b. Labor leader, Kate Dwyer

THURSDAY 14

1893 Paddy Hannan discovered gold in Kalgoorlie, WA

FRIDAY 15

SATURDAY 16

Last quarter of the moon 2.48 pm EST

SUNDAY 17

Corpus Christi
1952 d. artist, Ethel Carrick Fox
1958 b. ice skater, Robyn Burley

	June					
M	T	W	T	F	S	S
				1	2	3
4	5	6	7	8	9	10
11	12	13	14	15	16	17
18	19	20	21	22	23	24
25	26	27	28	29	30	

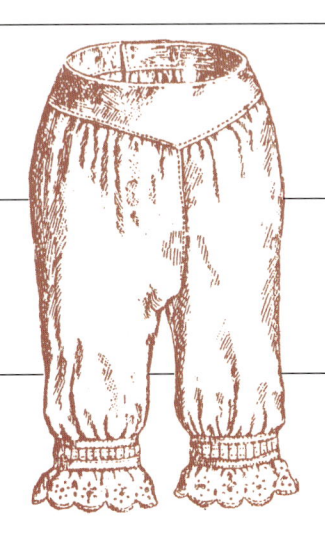

Headmistresses

CREATING THE MODERN AUSTRALIAN WOMAN

A century ago there were few occupations which 'respectable' women could enter into. However, teaching *was* one vocation which was open to women. There have been many strong-minded and intelligent women teachers and headmistresses who have played a significant role in the history of education in Australia – particularly in the education of women. Many headmistresses felt and stressed the need for girls to obtain a good education, in order that they be more independent in the rapidly developing world.

ELIZA FEWINGS

Eliza Anne Fewings (1857-1940) was born in Bristol. She trained as a teacher and after 8 years teaching she was appointed as headmistress of a girls' school in North Wales. In 1896 she left for Brisbane where she was to become headmistress of the Brisbane Girls' Grammar School.

In 1899 the second mistress of the school accused Eliza Fewings of academic incompetence and Miss Fewings was formally given notice. The announcement of her dismissal led to a furore of protest and two public meeting were held. The *Brisbane Courier* remarked that nothing but Federation had previously aroused such public interest.

After her dismissal from Brisbane Girls' Grammar School, Eliza immediately began her own school, the Brisbane State High School for Girls, later known as Somerville House. By 1903 it was the largest girls' school in Queensland, with 150 students. Miss Fewings, after much lobbying, finally secured external assessment through the Cambridge University Board of Examiners.

Eliza Fewings twice travelled overseas to keep herself informed about international educational developments. Her abilities were finally recognised and she became a member of the University Extension Committee, a member of the Council of the Brisbane Technical College and of the board of the Brisbane School of Arts.

In 1908 she returned to Wales to be the warden for women at a university college. She retired in 1914. In 1921 she returned to Brisbane for the twenty-first birthday of Somerville House and was herself honoured. She died in Wales at 83. Eliza Fewings was a woman of courage, high standards and energy.

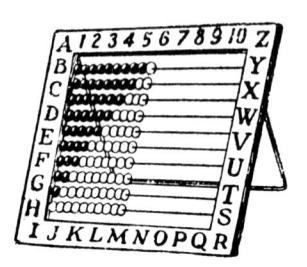

FANNY COHEN

Frances Cohen (1887-1975) was born in Grafton, New South Wales. She was educated at Miss Emily Baxter's Argyle School in Sydney and then at the University of Sydney, graduating with a Bachelor of Arts and of Science. She was awarded the Barker graduate scholarship to Cambridge University but her studies there were interrupted by her mother's illness.

In 1912, Fanny was appointed as mathematics teacher at Fort Street Girls' High School and became mathematics mistress in 1913. Later, she became deputy headmistress of North Sydney Girls' High School (1922), headmistress of Maitland Girls' High (1922), headmistress of St George Girls' High (1926) and headmistress of Fort Street Girls' High from 1929 until she retired in 1952.

Fort Street Girls' High was a selective school and the pupils were encouraged to aspire to university degrees and professional occupations. Fanny Cohen believed that girls were capable of attaining the same high academic standards as boys and could hold their own in any of the professions.

In 1934-44 and 1949-59, Fanny Cohen was a fellow of the Senate of the University of Sydney. She represented it on the Council of Women's College from 1936 and as a director of the Sydney University Women's Union in 1953-59.

In her retirement she helped the Royal Blind Society, learning braille and teaching it to sighted people who were to translate books into braille.

Fanny Cohen was an exceptional teacher and an outstanding headmistress. She died in 1975.

WINIFRED WEST

Winifred Mary West was born on 21 December 1881 in Frensham, Surrey, England. At Cambridge University she studied medieval and modern languages and excelled at hockey.

When she arrived in Sydney in 1907, she worked as an illustrator for the Australian Museum and was a pupil at Julian Ashton's famous art school. Winifred also convened the inaugural meeting of the New South Wales Women's Hockey Association in 1908.

In 1913 Winifred West established a girls' boarding school in Mittagong, called Frensham. She was headmistress until 1939.

Frensham had an experimental and enriched curriculum with an emphasis on the arts and physical education. The philosophy of the school was a reflection of Winifred West's own personal ideas and background. She was concerned with the image of the independent, modern Australian woman.

Winifred encouraged the girls to be responsible and cooperative rather than competitive. The reward for individual achievement was an iris. Frensham, as well as the other schools founded by Winifred, fostered, in her own words, 'the creative spirit'.

Winifred West was awarded an OBE in 1953. She remained a critic of the education system in which she felt there was 'little room for original work and imaginative thinking'.

Winifred West died in 1971.

WHAT WE WORE SKIING

It really is so long ago since we paid our first visits to Kosciusko; 1910, 11 and 12. The first year there was really a lot of snow, far below the Hotel, and very deep, almost up the window ledges; the lake was frozen, and we skated on it. Only one of our party had skied before; she was not very good, but had proper boots and skis, with bindings – very frustrating, as all we had were gumboots. Whenever anything happened, which was just about all the time, both skis invariably shot off in different directions, and had to be retrieved by plunging through the snow. But we had come to ski, and ski we did. We had a book called *How to Ski* and we did what it said, even to building jumps, and going over them, because the book said so. No one got really hurt either.

On looking at the old photographs, it is hard to believe how we managed at all; we were all in ankle-length skirts, and everything we wore was woolly, and just accumulated more and more snow, all the time. The skirts got slightly shorter according to the later photographs, but only to mid-calf.

Helen Rutledge, *My Grandfather's House*, 1986

June

MONDAY 18

1881 National Gallery of SA opened
1887 b. mining company director and welfare worker, Deborah Hackett
1920 b. poet, Rosemary Dobson
1948 b. performer, Robyn Archer

TUESDAY 19

1885 b. Adela Pankhurst Walsh, political activist and daughter of suffragette, Emmeline Pankhurst
1941 b. first head of NSW Department of Aboriginal Affairs, Pat O'Shan

WEDNESDAY 20

1863 d. ethnographer, Eliza Dunlop
1899 Perth's Royal Mint opened
1969 Arbitration Court accepted principle of equal pay for women

THURSDAY 21

1931 d. singer and actress, Nellie Stewart
1982 Qld Art Gallery opened in Brisbane

FRIDAY 22

Longest day
Winter solstice 1.33 am EST
1932 b. actress, June Salter
1977 Uniting Church in Australia officially inaugurated

SATURDAY 23

New moon 4.55 am EST

SUNDAY 24

International Women's Day for Peace and Disarmament
Birthday of St John the Baptist
1951 b. runner, Raelene Boyle

			June			
M	T	W	T	F	S	S
				1	2	3
4	5	6	7	8	9	10
11	12	13	14	15	16	17
18	19	20	21	22	23	24
25	26	27	28	29	30	

Leaves from a July Notebook

We are having such a cold winter here. At least we consider it cold. We have had quite sharp white frosts early in the morning and then a brilliant sunny day but with a sting in the air, as dear old Mr Ball used to say. One morning the pump was actually frozen!

It is warmer again now, and I hope we have done with the frosts. Strangely enough, I am perfectly well when the thermometer stands at 90° in the shade, but I have never been free from colds since the winter began. I am probably the only person in Queensland who wishes the summer back again. One morning it was so cold that we were fairly driven out of doors. There was a sharp south-west wind blowing hard, and a very creditable imitation it is, for a colony, of an English north-easter. It came into the house at every point, made the fire smoke and chilled the marrow of our bones. [1865]

David Adams (ed.), *The Letters of Rachel Henning*, 1969

June July

MONDAY 25

1852 First settlement of Gundagai wiped out by flood

TUESDAY 26

WEDNESDAY 27

1890 b. swimmer, Mina Wylie

THURSDAY 28

1836 One inch of snow fell in Sydney
1919 Signing of the Treaty of Versailles which ended World War I

FRIDAY 29

1918 b. art dealer and entrepreneur, Anne von Bertouch
1929 b. singer, June Bronhill

SATURDAY 30

First quarter of the moon 8.07 am EST
End of tax year
1885 b. ambulance driver, Olive King
1972 Ord River Dam officially opened

SUNDAY 1

1851 Victoria became a separate colony
1909 First Commonwealth old-age pension paid
1932 ABC formed
1961 b. Princess of Wales

	June					
M	T	W	T	F	S	S
				1	2	3
4	5	6	7	8	9	10
11	12	13	14	15	16	17
18	19	20	21	22	23	24
25	26	27	28	29	30	

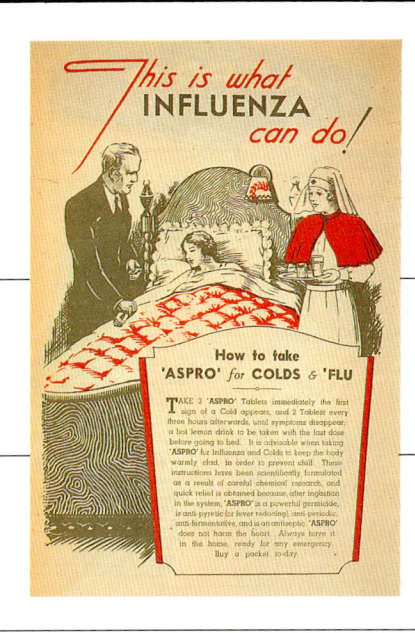

The Cancer Birthday
21 JUNE – 22 JULY

The symbol for Cancer is the Crab, and Cancer rules the stomach and digestion. It corresponds with the fourth house in the horoscope, which stands for home, parents, and young children.

The most typical thing about a Cancer person's appearance is usually the pallor of the skin, which has a white and transparent quality. Some Cancer folks are tall and slim, but other, more typical sorts, have top-heavy bodies, wider at the shoulders than at the hips, and they have a rolling or swaying walk. When a Cancerite sits, he or she frequently turns the toes in.

Cancer complaints are stomach troubles, weak digestion, and defective circulation.

The Cancer word is 'Hush!'

Aspro Year Book, 1936

THE KELLERMANS' DARING DAUGHTER

The Kellermans had a daughter about our age. She'd had infantile paralysis as a child and her devoted parents were advised to take her every day to bathe in the sea to exercise her limbs. Not only had she recovered, but had learned to swim like a fish. Mother played cards with her parents while we gazed pop-eyed at Annette, who'd just returned from England, where she'd challenged even *male* competitors. Her name was on everyone's lips – not because of her swimming prowess but because she was pioneering a new one-piece bathing costume without sleeves and reaching only to the knees.

Eugénie McNeil and Eugénie Crawford, *Ladies Didn't*, 1984

July

MONDAY 2

TUESDAY 3

St Thomas' Day

WEDNESDAY 4

1881 b. writer, Helena Sumner Locke, author of *Mum Dawson, Boss*

THURSDAY 5

1822 Royal Agricultural Society of NSW formed
1851 Vic. goldrush began at Anderson's Creek

FRIDAY 6

Alice Springs Show Day
1886 b. swimmer and film star, Annette Kellerman
1916 b. artist, Elizabeth Durack
1925 b. actress, Ruth Cracknell

SATURDAY 7

SUNDAY 8

Full moon 11.23 am EST

	July					
M	T	W	T	F	S	S
30	31					1
2	3	4	5	6	7	8
9	10	11	12	13	14	15
16	17	18	19	20	21	22
23	24	25	26	27	28	29

Annette Kellerman

Australian Children's Writers

TELL ME A STORY

Many of Australia's greatest and best-loved children's books have been written by women. Early this century, a number of Australian women writers achieved fame and fortune down this literary avenue. *Dot and the Kangaroo*, *Seven Little Australians* and *A Little Bush Maid* are probably three of the greatest Australian children's classics. Here we feature their creators.

Ethel Turner

ETHEL TURNER

Ethel Sibyl Turner was born in Doncaster, England in 1872. Her father died when she was young and her mother remarried a widower with six children. After Ethel's stepfather died, she, her mother and her stepsister emigrated to Sydney where her mother again remarried.

Ethel was educated at Sydney Girls' High School where she began a literary magazine entitled the *Iris*. This was superseded by the *Parthenon* (1889-1892) which stimulated her gift for children's writing. Some of her pieces were later used in the *Illustrated Sydney News* when she became editor of the children's column. She also contributed to the *Bulletin* as Dame Durdon.

In 1893 Ethel wrote her first and most famous children's book *Seven Little Australians*. The sequel, *The Family at Misrule*, followed in 1895. In total, Ethel wrote 27 full length novels, mostly for children, which were widely read both in Australia and overseas.

Ethel married H. R. Curlewis (later Judge) in 1896. She wrote from their Sydney home until her death in 1958.

There have been over 40 editions of *Seven Little Australians* and it has been translated into ten languages. It was made into a stage play (1915), a film (1939), and was televised in 1953 and 1973 by the BBC and ABC respectively.

ETHEL PEDLEY AND
Dot and the Kangaroo

Ethel Pedley was born in Acton, England, in 1860. Her family emigrated to Australia due to her father's ill health. Ethel, a talented musician, studied in Sydney, and gave several public concerts before returning to London for further musical studies. In 1881, however, she was forced to return to Australia's warm climate due to her own ailing health.

Back in Sydney Ethel taught music. She also gave more public concerts, performing herself or conducting. Ethel wrote the libretto for a cantata entitled *The Captive Soul* for which Emmeline Woolley had written the music. It was first performed in 1895 and proved very popular.

Dot and the Kangaroo was published in London in 1899. It had immediate success and is now considered a classic of Australian children's literature.

Dot, the daughter of an outback settler, becomes lost in the bush. A kindly red kangaroo, who has lost her joey, finds and befriends Dot. After many adventures in the bush, the kangaroo takes Dot safely back home. Dot's parents, who had thought her lost forever, promise never to shoot bush creatures again.

Often seen as an Australian *Alice in Wonderland*, *Dot and the Kangaroo* conveys a message about the conservation of Australian wildlife. In 1924 the book was adapted for the stage, and it was made into a film in 1977.

Ethel Pedley died when she was only 38 in 1898.

MARY GRANT BRUCE
(1878 – 1958)

Born and educated in Sale, Victoria, Mary (Minnie) Grant Bruce began writing at the age of seven. At 16 she won the essay competition of the Melbourne Shakespeare Society which she then won a further two times. She decided to become a journalist and also wrote fiction. Her first story *Her Little Lad* was published when she was 20.

Mary Grant Bruce worked on the staff of the *Age* for the children's page, contributing short stories, articles and serials. She also wrote for many other magazines and journals including *Woman's World*, *Woman* (both of which she edited) and the *Lone Hand*.

In the early 1900s she tried her hand at writing poetry, but when she heard it recited in public vowed never to attempt it again.

In 1905, *A Little Bush Maid* was serialised in the *Leader* and was published in book form in 1910. It was the first of her famous Billabong books, centred around a fictional station in northern Victoria, the home of the Linton family. The Billabong series of books ran until 1942. It made Mary one of the most famous Australian authors of her time and sold approximately two million copies.

Mary travelled to England in 1913 and wrote for the *Daily Mail*. She married her second cousin, George Bruce, who was also a writer.

In 1939 they again returned to Victoria. Mary spent her last years in Bexhill-on-Sea, Sussex, and she died in 1958.

Mary Grant Bruce

THE WONDER OF ELECTRICITY

The gas lights, I remember, had incandescent mantles on most of the brackets, but we were soon to get electric light. As the house was so newly built, my father was not prepared to rip up the walls and skirting boards to get it laid on, so many light switches were turned on by pulling a string from the ceiling. All the too few power plugs were attached clumsily on wood blocks and screwed on. Appliances were slow in coming on the market and radiators gave little more heat than foot warmers.

The electric iron and the vacuum cleaner were the first of the boons. No more maids to be seen strewing wet tea leaves or torn up pieces of paper on carpets to gather the dust when they swept the floor with millet brooms. Strangely enough, I do not remember us getting a refrigerator. I remember clearly the ice chest that held two blocks of ice and the iceman calling every other day. As we had a larder and fresh milk every day and fresh everything else brought to the door, there was no need to keep all the things people keep in refrigerators today for want of anywhere else to keep them.

Edith was one of the first to get a refrigerator. It was too large to be put in the kitchen and was placed on the back verandah. Its outside was made of wood, like an ice chest, and had a multitude of doors. Curious ladies, after dinner, were taken to the back premises to view the wonder.

Helen Rutledge, *My Grandfather's House*, 1986

July

MONDAY 9

1791 Third Fleet began arriving, bringing with them the first Irish conv
1897 b. politician and writer, Dame Enid Lyons

TUESDAY 10

1907 Sydney to Melbourne telephone line opened
1911 Royal Australian Navy established

WEDNESDAY 11

1846 b. founder of St Margaret's Hospital, Mother Abbott (Gertrude Abbott)
1863 Electric lighting first used at Observatory Hill and GPO, Sydney, to celebrate the marriage of the Prince of Wales

THURSDAY 12

1958 d. writer, Mary Grant Bruce, author of the *Billabong* series
1986 d. paediatrician, Kate Campbell

FRIDAY 13

Take care! Second Friday 13 this year!
Tennant Creek Show Day
1938 b. composer, Ann Carr-Boyd
1974 Dame Joan Sutherland first appeared with the Australian Opera

SATURDAY 14

SUNDAY 15

Last quarter of the moon 9.04 pm EST
1965 The *Australian* began publication in Canberra
1982 d. actress, Enid Lorimer

		July				
M	T	W	T	F	S	S
30	31					1
2	3	4	5	6	7	8
9	10	11	12	13	14	15
16	17	18	19	20	21	22
23	24	25	26	27	28	29

MARY ANN BAKER
BUSHRANGER

The daughter of an Aboriginal woman and a convict shepherd, Mary Ann Baker was born near Berrico, NSW. It was probably during the 1840s that Mary Ann met Fred Ward (later known as Captain Thunderbolt, the bushranger) when he was employed as a stockman around Berrico. In 1856 Captain Thunderbolt was arrested for horse stealing and sentenced to imprisonment at Cockatoo Island. He escaped with Mary Ann's help.

Mary Ann accompanied Captain Thunderbolt in his bushranging life in northern NSW and had at least three children by him. Mary Ann would dress as a man and, riding astride a horse, would steal cattle from a mob and kill it. The family's diet was mainly meat, supplemented with wild yams and wattle gum.

In 1886 Mary Ann and her children were caught by the police. She was described as 'a very smart woman, intelligent' who could 'read and write'. Little is known about her later life. It seems she may have used the death of another Aboriginal woman who was abandoned by Captain Thunderbolt as an opportunity to escape the police. Mary Ann returned to her father's home and may have later lived at Mudgee as the wife of a station hand called John Burrows, where she raised a large family. She died in 1905.

July

MONDAY 16

1942 b. tennis player, Margaret Court

TUESDAY 17

1902 b. writer, Christina Stead, author of *The Man Who Loved Children*

WEDNESDAY 18

1804 b. artist, Elizabeth Gould
1874 b. Catholic nun and educationalist, Catherine Forbes
1893 b. politician, May Holman
1925 b. athlete, Shirley de la Hunty

THURSDAY 19

1884 b. music publisher, Louise Dyer

FRIDAY 20

Katherine Show Day
1812 b. writer and artist, Louisa Meredith
1929 b. Hazel Hawke
1969 Humans first walked on the moon

SATURDAY 21

1898 Sydney's Queen Victoria Building was opened

SUNDAY 22

New moon 12.54 pm EST
St Mary Magdalen's Day

	July					
M	T	W	T	F	S	S
30	31					1
2	3	4	5	6	7	8
9	10	11	12	13	14	15
16	17	18	19	20	21	22
23	24	25	26	27	28	29

SICK FANCIES

The home nurse requires plenty of tact and firmness. She is very apt to give way to sick fancies, and, of course, it is very difficult to say 'no' to any of one's family. Where children are concerned this is often most trying for they have not sufficient sense to know that certain things are not good for them, and are withheld for that purpose. The nurse should have a light, firm tread.

The tapping of high heeled shoes is the limit, while squeaking shoes are past endurance. Bedroom slippers are no good for working in, besides which they are most 'sloppy' and tiring to the back. Quietness is the first essential, but this must not be confounded with gloom. Let the amateur nurse guard against knocking the end of the leg of the bed each time she moves round, and be careful against dropping scissors or pencil. And above all follow out the orders of the doctor to the very letter.

Sydney Mail, June 1914

HEALTH HINTS

Old people should avoid reading much by artificial light, be guarded as to diet, and avoid sitting up late at night.

After fifty bathe the eyes twice daily with water so hot that you wonder how you stand it; follow this with cold water that will make them glow with warmth.

The Dawn, March 1895

July

MONDAY 23

1964 d. founder member and first president of the CWA, Grace Munro
1986 Sarah Ferguson married Prince Andrew

TUESDAY 24

WEDNESDAY 25

1880 b. soprano, Amy Castles
1889 b. singer and founder of the Arts Council of Australia, Dorothy Helmrich

THURSDAY 26

Sts Joachim's and Anne's Day (parents of Mary)
1844 d. Anna King, wife of Governor King

FRIDAY 27

Darwin Show Day
1942 Australian Women's Land Army founded

SATURDAY 28

1901 b. writer, Henrietta Drake-Brockman, author of *The Wicked and the F*
1908 b. politician, Dame Annabelle Rankin
1934 d. anti-war activist, scholar and philanthropist, Marian Harwood

SUNDAY 29

1902 b. botanist and writer, Thistle Yolette Harris
1950 b. actress, Wendy Hughes
1981 Lady Diana Spencer married Prince Charles

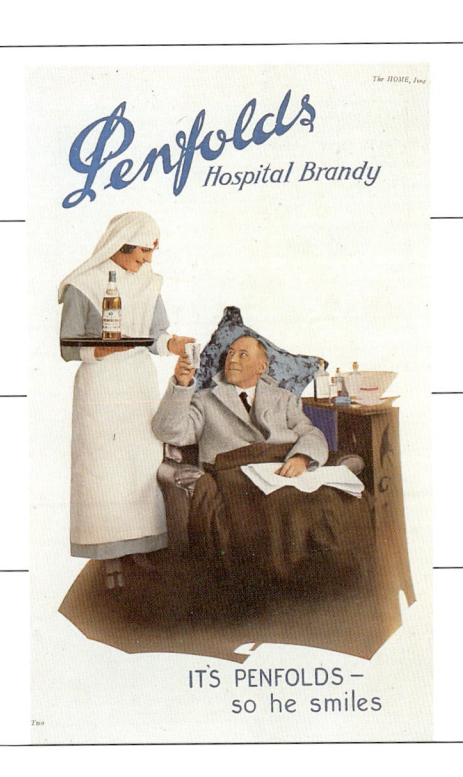

		July				
M	T	W	T	F	S	S
30	31					1
2	3	4	5	6	7	8
9	10	11	12	13	14	15
16	17	18	19	20	21	22
23	24	25	26	27	28	29

Women Botanical Artists

Painting and drawing were extremely popular occupations for cultured ladies of the past – botanical painting, in particular. Australia, a new and unexplored land, full of exotic and unidentified flora, was a haven for botanical painters among our early settlers. These painters avidly documented every fascinating new bloom they discovered. Often, they braved harsh and uncharted terrain in order that they might find that one elusive flower they had not yet captured on canvas. Ellis Rowan, Louisa Ann Meredith and Lady Margaret Forrest are three women who were talented painters, keen botanists and adventurers, who gained a lifetime's work and pleasure from the 'domestic hobby' of botanical painting.

Gigantic Lily, Ellis Rowan

LOUISA ANN MEREDITH

Born in Birmingham in 1812, Louisa Ann Meredith was brought up to be independent in her thinking and forthright in her speech. Louisa became an accomplished miniaturist with a great love of flowers.

In 1839 she married her cousin Charles Meredith, and they sailed to New South Wales. Later in 1840 they moved to Oyster Bay, Tasmania.

In 1844 Louisa wrote *Notes and Sketches of New South Wales,* which contained her shrewd and frank observations. It provoked angry reviews in Sydney but was widely read. In 1850 she wrote *My Home in Tasmania*. Her descriptions of the natural environment were thought to be among the best of their kind and they remain a valuable source for historians.

Native Wildflowers, Louisa Meredith

Besides her social commentaries, Louisa was also a writer of fiction and poetry.

Her paintings of the local flowers and animals, accompanied by her poetry, proved extremely popular, both in Australia and overseas. Louisa went on many excursions to study the flora and fauna of Tasmania. She corresponded with other leading naturalists, was an honorary member of the Royal Society of Tasmania and active in the RSPCA.

Her beautiful paintings of flowers and fish won her many prizes in Australia and internationally. In 1884 the Tasmanian government granted her a pension for 'distinguished literary and artistic services to the colony'. She died in 1895.

LADY MARGARET FORREST

Born in 1844 as Margaret Elvire Hammersley, Margaret Forrest settled with her family at the Swan River Colony (now Perth) in 1837.

In 1876 she married John Forrest, who was later to become Western Australia's first premier. Her position in society, together with her great interest in the native fauna, led her to work with many leading botanists and botanical artists who visited Western Australia. In 1880 Lady Margaret provided specimens for the English botanical artist, Marianne North, when she visited Australia. Lady Margaret also toured Geraldton and the area north of Carnarvon with Ellis Rowan in 1889, to paint the spring flowers.

Lady Margaret Forrest was a founding member of the West Australian Society of Arts (1896) and of the Wilgie Club. She died in 1929.

ELLIS ROWAN

Marian Ellis Rowan was born in 1848 in Victoria where she was brought up. She had no formal art training, apart from the watercolour classes at Miss Murphy's High School for Girls. Ellis married Captain Frederick Rowan in 1873.

Ellis lacked neither élan nor courage. She spent much of her time travelling the wilder parts of the world in search of specimens to paint, encountering crocodiles, tarantulas, giant lizards and natives. She braved the tropical scrubs and wilderness of Queensland, right up to Cape York Peninsula.

Captain Rowan died in 1895 and, although heartbroken, Ellis continued to work hard. In 1895 she had a very successful exhibition of watercolours in London and was invited to meet Queen Victoria. The London press saw Ellis as an extraordinary and exotic creature, much like the flora and fauna she was wont to paint.

In her search for wildflowers and birds, she travelled to America where she met Alice Lounsberry, a botanist. The two women spent 12 years together, travelling and illustrating flora and fauna for various publications, including their own.

Ellis Rowan was a prolific artist who produced approximately 3000 pictures. She won many medals and prizes for her work which, however, was only taken seriously towards the end of her life.

Ellis Rowan, painter, writer, botanist, explorer and adventurer, wrought an international reputation and a full and exciting life from what was often regarded as the 'petty' and 'female' art of flower painting.

Leaves from an August Notebook

We have been down here more than two months now, and I have never taken out an umbrella since we came. The dust is as bad as in the height of summer, and winter clothes show it so much that we are always brushing.

We have had a great deal of cold wind. Nevertheless, the days have been bright and beautiful, and the flowers are coming out in the bush. I often take Teddy for a walk on the wild hills that lie between Randwick and Botany. They are low hills of white sand, and are covered with low-growing shrubs and flowers of all descriptions. There are also a great many flowers in the garden – geraniums and petunias and hyacinths and jonquils.

[1872]

David Adams (ed.), *The Letters of Rachel Henning*, 1969

THE 'CUT DIRECT'

The 'cut direct' which is given by a prolonged stare at a person, if justified at all, can only be in case of extraordinary and notoriously bad conduct on the part of the individual 'cut,' and is very seldom called for. If any one wishes to avoid a bowing acquaintance with another, it can be done by looking aside or dropping the eyes. It is an invariable rule of good society, that a gentleman cannot 'cut' a lady under any circumstances, but circumstances may arise when he may be excused for persisting in not meeting her eyes, for if their eyes meet, he must bow.

Australian Etiquette, 1885

July August

MONDAY 30

First quarter of the moon 12.01 am EST
1848 b. flower painter, Ellis Rowan

TUESDAY 31

1895 Art Gallery of WA established
1941 b. squash player, Heather McKay
1951 b. tennis player, Evonne Goolagong-Cawley

WEDNESDAY 1

1840 Transportation of convicts to NSW ceased
1902 *New Idea* first published
1914 World War I declared
1984 The *Sex Discrimination Act* came into force

THURSDAY 2

1861 b. politician and social worker, Edith Cowan

FRIDAY 3

SATURDAY 4

1914 Australia entered World War I
1958 d. writer and poet, Ethel Anderson, author of *Indian Tales*

SUNDAY 5

1859 d. pastoralist, Eliza Forlonge
1944 Cowra Breakout

August

M	T	W	T	F	S	S
	1	2	3	4	5	
6	7	8	9	10	11	12
13	14	15	16	17	18	19
20	21	22	23	24	25	26
27	28	29	30	31		

AUSTRALIA — THE TELEGRAPH MESSENGER

The Leo Birthday
23 JULY – 22 AUGUST

The symbol for the sign Leo is a Lion, and Leo rules the heart in the human body. Leo corresponds with the fifth house of the horoscope, and stands for kingship and authority, love, children, speculation, and the stage.

You can tell a Leo type by the florid complexion or high colouring, but don't forget that Aries and Sagittarius types also tend to this complexion, so it is not an infallible Leo sign. Leo people have an erect, dignified walk, with a buoyant step, and their eyes are possibly their most typical feature. Many of them have large, beautiful eyes, often blue or grey, sometimes full and staring in expression, but certain Leo types have weak sight or a slight cast in one eye, and they tend to wear pince-nez, usually of the rimless kind. Leo people also frequently have large, strong-looking teeth. Sometimes they look sideways like a cat.

The typical Leo complaint is heart palpitation. Leos break all the known rules of health and physical fitness, and get away with it, at least for a long time.

The Leo word is 'Oh!' and the motto 'Aristocratic power!'

Aspro Year Book, 1936

August

MONDAY 6
Hiroshima Day
Transfiguration of the Lord
Bank holiday, NSW, ACT
Picnic Day, NT

TUESDAY 7
Full moon 12.19 am EST
Partial lunar eclipse at 11 am EST – visible from all Australia
1912 Akubra hat first registered

WEDNESDAY 8
1909 d. Sister Mary McKillop

THURSDAY 9
Brisbane Exhibition begins

FRIDAY 10
1857 Melbourne first lit with gas
1931 NSW first lottery drawn with a prize of £5000
1987 Lecki Ord became the first woman Lord Mayor of Melbourne

SATURDAY 11
1915 d. preacher and suffragette campaigner, Martha Webster
1920 b. politician, Lady Florence Bjelke-Petersen

SUNDAY 12
1829 Perth founded and named after the town in Scotland
1920 d. writer and founder of the *Dawn*, Louisa Lawson

August						
M	T	W	T	F	S	S
		1	2	3	4	5
6	7	8	9	10	11	12
13	14	15	16	17	18	19
20	21	22	23	24	25	26
27	28	29	30	31		

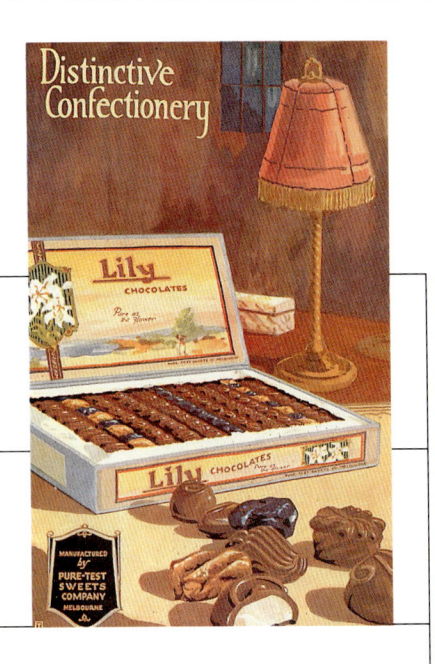

IS WOMAN LOSING HER CHARM?

Because we no longer depend on man for the needs of life, but go out and fight for them on common ground, we are, forsooth, losing our charm, our sex appeal, our femininity – misused term – in fact, we are 'unsexed' creatures who put a bigger value on personal success than on spreading our nets, with simpering hypocrisy, to ensnare the simple male...

The frank, comradely girl of to-day, with her eagerness for life and all that life can give is a much more charming creature than her Victorian prototype, who was a mass of affectations, and whose reputation for the evasive thing called charm, depended on her helplessness, her 'clinging vine' propensities, her girlish gush and her sheltered 'innocence,' rather than on the fascination of character...

In herself the woman who earns her own salt and can talk to men about the things that interest men, is an infinitely more attractive individual than the woman who threw a fit of hysterics on the slightest provocation and could not have earned a shilling had her life depended on it.

Her 'charm' is of the enduring kind that will make her a real companion to her husband and a good pal to her children when they come to the rough places in life.

Helen's Weekly, November 1927

August

MONDAY 13

1898 Australian Army Nursing Service began in NSW
1919 First public demonstration of radio broadcasting
1941 Australian Women's Army Service formed

TUESDAY 14

Last quarter of the moon 1.54 am EST
1956 d. composer, May Brahe

WEDNESDAY 15

Assumption of the Virgin
1920 b. artist, Judy Cassab
1950 b. Princess Anne

THURSDAY 16

1865 b. poet, Dame Mary Gilmore
1897 b. writer, Marjorie Barnard, author of *The Persimmon Tree and Other S*

FRIDAY 17

1980 Nine-week-old Azaria Chamberlain went missing from her parents' tent at a campsite near Ayers Rock

SATURDAY 18

Brisbane Exhibition ends
1885 b. writer and poet, Nettie Palmer

SUNDAY 19

M	T	W	T	F	S	S
		1	2	3	4	5
6	7	8	9	10	11	12
13	14	15	16	17	18	19
20	21	22	23	24	25	26
27	28	29	30	31		

August

Amateur Theatricals

A MOST GRACEFUL AMUSEMENT

Private theatricals are more than a mere intellectual play; they may range from a trivial amusing dialogue in character, to the drawing-room drama, which has elicited the intellectual gifts of Moore, Sheridan, or Charles Dickens. There are dangers connected with it, as with most other amusements, but with some kindly observer or judicious friend to supervise the proceedings, it is a most graceful amusement, calculated to stimulate the mind, to give ease of manner and graceful elocution, and to make young people seek wider charms of mutual sympathy, and these highest of all pleasures which are intellectual. In choosing plays for the drawing-room stage, care should be taken not to attempt too much.

The modern lyrical drama is a favourite, though it is beyond the range of amateur actors, and the mimic scene ill replaces the glittering effects of modern theatres.

Rehearsals should be carefully attended to, no indulgence in personal whims or preferences should be allowed, but the directions of the stage-manager, who should be, if not a professional actor, at least competent for the work, should in all cases be rigidly attended. There is no greater proof of good sense and sweet disposition, than to pass the ordeal of taking part in amateur theatricals without a single quarrel.

Australian Etiquette, 1885

MAKING-UP

Amateurs require, if anything, greater care in 'Making-up' than Professionals, as their audiences consist mostly of their personal and intimate friends. Consequently, if they are not well 'made-up', the moment they make their appearance on the stage they are greeted, *sotto voce*, with the exclamations 'There he is!' 'There's Charlie!' 'That's Harry!' or similar remarks, and during the whole performance, no matter how well they may perform, they appear merely as 'Charlie' and 'Harry'.

Death
As the scenes in which deaths occur are of a highly impressive nature, and as the success, perhaps, of the whole piece depends upon their being effectively rendered, great care and nicety must be employed when 'making-up' the face to give it a ghastly, death-like appearance, in order not to destroy the illusion by overdoing it...

First powder the face and throat well with the Prepared Whiting, afterwards with a hare's foot apply a good colouring of Dutch pink...

Americans
As a rule, when an American is represented on the English stage both dress and 'Make-up' are to some extent exaggerated.

Ladies
Ladies, as a rule, are so perfect in the art of improving their looks and rendering themselves handsome that to offer them any advice on *that* subject would be simply useless...

How to 'Make-up', A Practical Guide for Amateurs &c., 1877

SONG OF THE CITIES

I have a hazy memory of Helen Onslow (Lady Stanham) being enthroned as Britannia, Union Jacks, trident and all, and that the Empire was upheld by the *Song of the Cities*; each city was represented by a lovely girl who came on, bowed or salaamed to Britannia and declaimed the appropriate four-line verse from that poem and then struck and held an attitude of some kind.

The Kelly family at that time was living at Caerleon, across the road from Llanillo, and I remember going there several times to be rehearsed by Mrs Kelly in the part of Madras. I was seemingly unable to remember my lines, and when on stage, 'dried up' completely. So Mrs Kelly spoke the lines from the wings, with greater clarity than I could have managed. Afterwards, all I could remember of the verse I could not bring myself to utter, was 'A withered beldame, now.' I would be no more able to recite it today...

Two other girls were memorable because they had speech impediments. Singapore began and ended on one long hiss with, 'East and West must seek my aid', and Auckland lisped her way through, 'Last, loneliest, loveliest, most exquisite and apart'.

Helen Rutledge, *My Grandfather's House*, 1986

BRISBANE

I am very pleased with Brisbane, it is so picturesque from the river. There are some excellent shops and some quite handsome buildings. Last week Walter took me for a pull up the river past the Botanic Gardens. It was so lovely. The day before yesterday he brought home a young fellow from the office, Spicer Briggs, and they pulled me down the river which is really pretty. We saw some patches of sugar plantation. What I admire most are the tufts of Bamboo which grow like gigantic ferns. There are bananas in every garden, they also look like ferns for their broad handsome leaves get split into a fringe by the wind, it is only the young leaves which are entire. When we came back from our row we sauntered to a pretty wild spot close by where the bank of the river is high and rocky and thence had a glorious view of the city and river which is very winding. The sun was setting behind the dark hills which made a background to the panorama. How I longed for you all to see it. The atmosphere is so intensely clear here, it gives a new beauty to everything. As we sit on the verandah at night the river and the city on the opposite shore look so very beautiful with the lights reflected in the water and stars shining so brightly overhead.

Katie Fowler, 1866

August

MONDAY 20

New moon 10.39 pm EST
1946 b. ballet dancer, Marilyn Rowe-Maver

TUESDAY 21

1907 b. Betty Archdale, Headmistress of Abbotsleigh, woman cricketer Principal of the Women's College at the University of Sydney

WEDNESDAY 22

1972 d. writer, Ernestine Hill, author of *My Love Must Wait*

THURSDAY 23

1937 b. Franca Arena, first woman from a non-English speaking background to enter Australian Parliament

FRIDAY 24

1951 b. singer, Julie Anthony
1968 d. artist, Kate O'Connor

SATURDAY 25

1925 b. writer, Thea Astley, author of *A Descant for Gossips*

SUNDAY 26

1768 Captain Cook's ship the *Endeavour* left Plymouth on its voyage of discovery to Australia
1901 b. writer, Eleanor Dark, author of *The Timeless Land*

August						
M	T	W	T	F	S	S
		1	2	3	4	5
6	7	8	9	10	11	12
13	14	15	16	17	18	19
20	21	22	23	24	25	26
27	28	29	30	31		

BRISBANE Q.
PARLIAMENT HOUSE

Leaves from a September Notebook

We have such beautiful flowers out in the creek now. The fire-tree, we used to call it last year. It is a small tree covered with beautiful crimson blossoms, bottle-brush-shaped as many of the Australian flowers are. All the wildflowers will be coming out soon...We have been here just a year this month. I can hardly fancy it, for it does not seem any time. Time flies so very fast in the bush. I suppose it is from the easy, free sort of life and from one day being much like another. [1863]

David Adams (ed.), *The Letters of Rachel Henning*, 1969

SPRING

Spring is announced by the smell of wattle, peppery and pervasive; and as elsewhere by the sound of birds in country and town. Even the magpie with its loud and liquid attack upon notes, a song of incomparable beauty, comes to the city and adds to the clamour of the early morning. The sky in springtime by night or day brings its highest plumes to trail across the blue.

Maie Casey, *An Australian Story 1837-1907*, 1962

August / September

MONDAY 27

1902 NSW granted female suffrage
1904 b. Gladys (Aunty Glad) Elphick

TUESDAY 28

First quarter of the moon 5.34 pm EST
1835 Melbourne founded
1985 AUSSAT launched

WEDNESDAY 29

Martyrdom of St John the Baptist
1849 Australia's first amateur women's golf tournament played at Geelong Vic. It was won by Miss C. B. Mackenzie

THURSDAY 30

1986 d. politician, Dame Annabelle Rankin

FRIDAY 31

Royal Adelaide Show begins
1830 b. physician and feminist, Harriet Clisby

SATURDAY 1

First day of spring
1910 b. ballet dancer and administrator, Dame Peggy van Praagh
1951 Australia, NZ and the US signed the ANZUS mutual defence pact
1976 Cigarette advertising banned on television and radio

SUNDAY 2

Father's Day
1939 Menzies announced Australia's entry into World War II
1948 d. community worker and politician, Margaret McIntyre in a plane crash

M	T	W	T	F	S	S
		1	2	3	4	5
6	7	8	9	10	11	12
13	14	15	16	17	18	19
20	21	22	23	24	25	26
27	28	29	30	31		

August

Father's Day

CHEERFULNESS AT THE TABLE

Children should not be prohibited from laughing and talking at the table. Joyousness promotes the circulation of the blood, enlivens and invigorates it, and sends it to all parts of the system, carrying with it animation, vigour and life. Controversy should not be permitted at the table, nor should any subjects which call forth political or religious difference. Every topic introduced should be calculated to instruct, interest or amuse. Business matters, past disappointments and mishaps should not be alluded to, nor should bad news be spoken of at the table, nor for half an hour before. All conversation should be of joyous and gladsome character, such as will bring out pleasant remarks and agreeable associations.

Australian Etiquette, 1885

TOM BECOMES A FATHER

As soon as the meal was over I had to throw my bombshell. He would have to fetch Mrs Jones the nurse, who had arranged to look after me and my nearest neighbour Mrs Kean, who lived at the Rabbit proof hut, four miles away. Of course hubby was horrified to think that I had been doing all that hard work all day, but he knew that the roof wouldn't have been on without my help...So he set off to walk. By 9 o'clock he was back alone. Mrs J. vowed that she couldn't safely leave Mrs Kean that night!...Very soon he returned with a rough sort of woman, but who appeared capable and good natured. I had gone to bed and things were becoming decidedly lively. She had a look at me and remarked cheerfully – 'You'll be a good deal worse before you're better' – and went and sat by the fire with Tom. She started to tell him what they both seemed to think a most amusing yarn...At last I called to her to come as the baby had arrived. 'Wait on', she said, 'I must finish the yarn' – which she did. Then she came and took the baby, saying it was just twenty past ten, and she would have to go back home soon. She and Tom went on talking and I called out 'Is it a he or a she, Mrs Holmes?' 'It's the finest little Navvy ever I've seen, and I can't get his fingers undone from my apron,' she said. 'Then, that's Arthur Thomas,' I said. 'My oath, that's the quickest named child ever I came across' was her reply. [Queensland 1892].

Constance Ellis, *I Seek Adventure*, 1981

TO PARENTS

While it is folly to try to make a finished performer of a girl with no natural bent toward music, it is perhaps a sin to allow her to grow up without some technical knowledge of what will refine her taste, enlarge her sympathies, and afford her lasting entertainment for weary and solitary hours. Many of us who never advanced much beyond five finger exercises realise that even our little familiarity with the piano and musical signs is priceless.

The Dawn, February 1895

The Virgo Birthday
23 AUGUST – 22 SEPTEMBER

The symbol for the sign Virgo is the Virgin Young Maiden, holding in her hand a few ears of wheat. This indicates that Virgo rules bread and foodstuffs in general, as well as many other things. Virgo corresponds with the sixth sign of the Zodiac, and stands for work, health, uncles and aunts. The part of the body ruled by Virgo is the area beneath the belt line, mainly the liver and intestines. You can pick out Virgo people in many cases by their medium height, wide shoulders, smallish heads, sharp or pointed, delicate features, and their slender, spare, and neat appearance, or by their neat, quiet dress, round faces, and quiet voices, which tend to become shrill when they get excited. The main feature is the fine forehead, often high, but sometimes bulging in a way that reminds one of a baby or young child's forehead.

The typical Virgo complaints are colic or bowel disturbances...You can seldom tell their age, and they usually look younger than they are.

The Virgo word is 'Don't!' the motto 'Efficiency – Reason.' No other birthday in the year is so clever at 'making both ends meet' as a Virgo.

Aspro Year Book, 1936

September

MONDAY 3

1901 Australian national flag flown for the first time. The flag was chose by the public
1926 *Canberra Times* first published

TUESDAY 4

1855 Lola Montez scandalised the goldfields with her 'spider dance'
1937 b. swimmer, Dawn Fraser

WEDNESDAY 5

Full moon 11.46 am EST

THURSDAY 6

1859 Municipality of Brisbane proclaimed

FRIDAY 7

1923 b. writer, Nancy Keesing

SATURDAY 8

Royal Adelaide Show ends
Birthday of the Virgin Mary
1900 b. madam, Tilly Devine

SUNDAY 9

1786 *The Times* first reported the despatch of convicts to Botany Bay
1883 b. politician, Millicent Preston Stanley
1909 b. athlete, Decima Norman

	September					
M	T	W	T	F	S	S
					1	2
3	4	5	6	7	8	9
10	11	12	13	14	15	16
17	18	19	20	21	22	23
24	25	26	27	28	29	30

105

KATHLEEN O'CONNOR

Kathleen (Kate) O'Connor is one of Australia's most important women artists. She was born in 1876 in Hokitika, New Zealand, the daughter of engineer, C. Y. O'Connor, who built the first 300-mile water pipeline to Kalgoorlie in Western Australia. In 1891 the family went to live in Perth.

Early in 1900 Kate joined art classes at Perth Technical School where she studied under James W. R. Linton. After leaving art school, she took a position as art mistress at a girls school. It was quite something for a woman of Kate's station to be working for a living.

In 1902 Kate O'Connor was listed as a working member of the West Australian Society of Arts. One of her drawings was exhibited in the annual exhibition that year and in 1903 she exhibited six pieces as well as some of her leatherwork. She was elected to the committee in 1904.

In 1906 Kate realised her ambition to go abroad. She lived in Paris, which she loved. She then studied art for a short time in England before being drawn again to Paris, where she finally settled in 1910.

Kate O'Connor exhibited her work at the Salon d'Automne (1911-32) and in the *Exposition des Femmes Artistes d'Europe* in 1937. She also had many other exhibitions. During World War II after losing her studio and many of her possessions she went to live in England. She finally settled in Perth again in 1955. By that time she had become very French in her attitude, habits and painting style.

She won the Perth Prize in 1958 and the BP Prize and Commonwealth Games art competition in 1962. Her works are in all state galleries, many regional galleries and some university collections.

September

MONDAY 10

1914 b. author and historian, Margaret Kiddle

TUESDAY 11

WEDNESDAY 12

Last quarter of the moon 6.53 am EST

THURSDAY 13

1901 The spectacular film and lantern slide show, *Soldiers of the Cross*, produced in Melbourne by the Salvation Army
1931 b. athlete, Marjorie Jackson, Olympic medal winner who broke ten world records between 1949 and 1954, known as the 'Lithgow Flash'

FRIDAY 14

Triumph of the Holy Cross
1876 b. artist, Kate O'Connor
1983 Jennie George became the first woman elected to the ACTU Executive

SATURDAY 15

1886 b. Labor activist, Mary Ryan

SUNDAY 16

1948 b. singer, Olivia Newton John
1956 Television began in Australia

	September					
M	T	W	T	F	S	S
					1	2
3	4	5	6	7	8	9
10	11	12	13	14	15	16
17	18	19	20	21	22	23
24	25	26	27	28	29	30

Australian Riches, Kathleen O'Connor

VIOLENT PASSION

He approached me and was stooping to kiss me. I cannot account for my action or condemn it sufficiently. It was hysterical – the outcome of an overstrung, highly excitable, and nervous temperament. Perhaps my vanity was wounded, and my tendency to strike when touched was up in arms. The calm air of ownership with which Harold drew near annoyed me, or, as Sunday-school teachers would explain it, Satan got hold of me. He certainly placed a long strong riding-whip on the table beneath my hand. As Harold stooped with the intention of pressing his lips to mine, I quickly raised the whip and brought it with all my strength right across his face. The instant the whip had descended I would have smashed my arm on the door-post to recall that blow. But that was impossible.

Miles Franklin, *My Brilliant Career*, 1901

♥

TALKING OF KISSES

In the first place, faint kisses never won any lady.

It's never too late to kiss. And a kiss in time saves nine situations out of ten.

Never ask a woman whether you may kiss her. And don't plead with her if she refuses. A woman has more respect for a man she has refused to kiss than for one whose kisses she merely submits to.

The kisses a woman gives you are beyond price. But if you have to pay anything at all for them they cost too much.

The reason most women refuse kisses is because they don't want them. And that's the one reason no man can believe.

Australian Woman's Mirror, October 1926

September

MONDAY 17

1879 Sydney's Botanic Gardens became the venue for Australia's first International Exhibition
1902 b. eccentric Sydney character, Bea Miles

TUESDAY 18

WEDNESDAY 19

Women's Suffrage Day
New moon 10.46 am EST
1838 First flower show held by Floral and Horticultural Society in Sydney
1954 d. writer, Miles Franklin, author of *My Brilliant Career*

THURSDAY 20

Royal Melbourne Show begins
Rosh Hashananah
1886 b. nurse, Sister Elizabeth Kenny

FRIDAY 21

St Matthew's Day

SATURDAY 22

1904 b. author, Dymphna Cusack, author of *Come in Spinner*
1921 Ladies' Golf Union of Australia founded

SUNDAY 23

Spring equinox 4.56 pm EST
1965 Roma Mitchell took up her position as first woman judge when she was appointed to the SA Bench

		September				
M	T	W	T	F	S	S
					1	2
3	4	5	6	7	8	9
10	11	12	13	14	15	16
17	18	19	20	21	22	23
24	25	26	27	28	29	30

I DREAM OF THE TIME WHEN OUR LIPS SHALL MEET IN LOVE'S FIRST KISS, DIVINELY SWEET!

The Australian Garden

Australia, a land of houses with backyards, is also a nation of keen gardeners. Let us have a look at some of the most influential gardeners of our past – who happen to be women – as well as some images of 'the Australian garden'.

. . .

JANET WATERHOUSE

Eryldene, in Gordon, Sydney, is a house which preserves the lives and works of professor E. G. Waterhouse and his wife Janet. Eryldene took its name from Janet Waterhouse's childhood home in Scotland.

Janet Waterhouse was as passionately interested in gardening as her husband, and while he became the expert on developing and breeding camellias, she played a vitally important part in the development of the garden at Eryldene. The couple shared wide ranging interests in languages, sculpture, painting and flowers and it was through these interests that Janet Waterhouse became involved in ikebana, the subtle and beautiful art of Japanese flower arranging. Her husband was Professor of Modern Languages at the University of Sydney and his colleagues brought Janet authentic bronze and bamboo ikebana containers from Japan. She began to experiment. In the 1950s, as president of the Garden Club of Australia, she met Norman Sparnon, an ikebana expert who had studied in Japan for many years. He was impressed by her arrangements, despite her lack of formal training, and she became his pupil. She loved the classical simplicity of ikebana and her sensitivity made her an excellent pupil.

Janet Waterhouse became the first president of the Sydney chapter of Ikebana International. She visited Japan and remained involved with ikebana until her death in 1973.

A LADY GARDENER

'My father thought I would be a boy and he went ahead with his preconceived ideas on "how to bring up a boy hardy".' Edna Walling's unconventional upbringing, for a girl born in the late 1890s, left her with an important legacy of skills and talents that made her one of Australia's most original landscape architects.

The Walling family emigrated to Australia from Devon when Edna was in her mid-teens. She enrolled in the Burnley Horticultural College, where she was 'a very fine student'. Several years later, she had developed a hatred of gardens, which she claimed 'grew deeper and deeper'. It was only when the idea came to her that she could become a *creator* of gardens, that her true vocation became clear.

She quickly showed her considerable talent as a landscaper. Prominent clients, including Dame Nellie Melba, helped make a Walling garden a status symbol. But it was her ability to break away from a formal garden style, to use plants and structures creatively and freely, that was the true source of her success.

One of the first landscapers to use native plants, she never lost her love of soft, English cottage gardens. When she died in 1973, she had written four books, hundreds of magazine articles and was the creator of a style of landscape architecture which is still influential today.

THAT FUGITIVE CHARM

It is a most elusive thing, this matter of design in the garden, and it is not always the fervent horticulturalist who achieves it. It is more often the person who builds a garden for the quiet peace and mental refreshment he hopes to find therein: a person with a good sense of proportion, and a subconscious understanding of the basic principles that have produced the loveliest gardens in the world. Admittedly, many a charming garden has been contrived without a full complement of these qualifications, but charm is a fugitive thing; and when winter comes, laying bare so much of the construction, it is sometimes a little distressing to look out upon a garden that is rather elementary in design when stripped of foliage and flowers.

Edna Walling

The Libra Birthday
23 SEPTEMBER – 22 OCTOBER

The symbol for the sign Libra is a Pair of Scales at even balance.

Libra rules the kidneys, the balancers of the body, and dizziness and loss of balance are signs of disordered kidneys. Libra corresponds with the seventh house in the horoscope, which rules marriage, partnership, and co-operation with others.

It is not easy to pick a Libra man or woman, because they are so harmonious that they don't tend to marked peculiarities. They are beautiful people, usually tall and slender, but tending to put on flesh to some extent in middle life. They have fine hair, often parted in the middle, and delicate skins.

The Libra word is 'Quite,' and the motto is 'Balance – Judgment.' The Libra typical complaints are kidney disorders and backaches.

Aspro Year Book, 1936

A CURE FOR INSOMNIA

'Curl yourself under the clothes like a kitten if at night you can't go to sleep,' says Dr. J. E. Huxley, of Maidstone. 'Lower the supply of oxygen in the blood, produce a little asphyxia, breathe and rebreathe only the respired air. You will then reduce the stimulating oxygen and fall asleep. There is no danger. When asleep you are sure to disturb the coverings and get the fresh air. When the cat and dog prepare to sleep they bury their nose in some hollow in their hair and "off" they go. Chloral is dangerous. The sleepless should try Nature's plan.'

The Dawn, December 1894

September

MONDAY 24

1923 b. Dame Beryl Beaurepaire, first Convenor of the National Women's Advisory Service (1978)
1929 b. writer, Barbara Ker Wilson, author of *Jane Austen in Australia*

TUESDAY 25

1942 b. actress, Robyn Nevin

WEDNESDAY 26

1909 b. artist, Elaine Haxton
1912 Presbyterian Inland Mission founded by the Reverend John Flynn to serve outback Australia

THURSDAY 27

First quarter of the moon 12.06 pm EST
Show Day holiday, Vic.
1932 Lores Bonney became first woman to fly around Australia. She took 43 days and spent 95 hours in the air

FRIDAY 28

1928 Melba's final opera performance
1934 Freda Thompson became first Australian woman to fly solo from England to Australia
1973 Opera Theatre of the Sydney Opera House opened

SATURDAY 29

Michael, Gabriel & Raphael, Archangels' Day
Perth Royal Show begins

SUNDAY 30

Royal Melbourne Show ends
1976 Final episode of Gwen Meredith's *Blue Hills*

September

M	T	W	T	F	S	S
					1	2
3	4	5	6	7	8	9
10	11	12	13	14	15	16
17	18	19	20	21	22	23
24	25	26	27	28	29	30

Leaves from an October Notebook

October 19th, Sunday afternoon (1862). Sunday seems so quiet in the bush. I should like to hear some church bells, but there is no bell near, except that on the blackboy's pony, which I hear tinkling somewhere in the bush.

It is a beautiful afternoon, the warm air blowing in through the open door and window, and whispering among the gumtrees, cloud shadows gliding over the opposite mountain range, great Lion, the bloodhound, lying asleep in the doorway, quite regardless of being walked or fallen over. Biddulph arrayed in white trousers, white coat and regatta shirt (nobody ever sits in the parlour without a coat) is lazily reading in an armchair in the pleasant recess where the books are. Mr Hedgeland in a similar airy costume is writing to his aunts, the Miss Hedgelands at Exeter, at the table. Annie, in a very pretty black and green mohair dress trimmed with green silk lozenges, is also writing – to Amy. Mr Taylor and Beckford, who came in last night, one from the Seven Mile, and the other from a station forty miles off, are sitting on the veranda discoursing.

Douglas Adams (ed.), *The Letters of Rachel Henning*, 1969

October

MONDAY 1

Labour Day, NSW, ACT
Queen's Birthday holiday, WA
1875 First Australian postcards went on sale at the Sydney GPO
1924 b. academic, Dame Leonie Kramer

TUESDAY 2

Guardian Angels' Day
1913 b. judge of the Supreme Court, Dame Roma Mitchell
1969 d. writer, Katherine Susannah Prichard, author of *Coonardoo*

WEDNESDAY 3

THURSDAY 4

Full moon 10.02 pm EST
St Francis of Assisi's Day
1922 d. flower painter, Ellis Rowan

FRIDAY 5

Burnie Show Day, Tas.
1932 b. actress, Diane Cilento

SATURDAY 6

Perth Royal Show ends
1789 The *Rose Bay Packet*, first ship built in Australia, launched

SUNDAY 7

1916 Sydney's Taronga Park Zoo officially opened

	October					
M	T	W	T	F	S	S
1	2	3	4	5	6	7
8	9	10	11	12	13	14
15	16	17	18	19	20	21
22	23	24	25	26	27	28
29	30	31				

The Love Story, E. Phillips Fox, 1903

THE GOOD OLD DAYS

Every girl knew that if she was tolerably pleasant she could be married. Beauty and grace had of course their peculiar attraction here as elsewhere, but a certain degree of usefulness combined with good temper was recognised as the chief recommendation for a wife. In the early days of the colonies a wife was not looked on as a hindrance or an expense, but as a help and a comfort. Girls did not look for establishments; parents did not press for settlements, a trousseau might cost £15 – it was handsome if it cost £25; there were no wedding presents, no cards; the cake might be made at home or dispensed with altogether. There was only one carriage in the colony for many years, which, though belonging to a private person, was hired for such as wanted to do the thing genteely…They began life with youth and love and hope and trust, and what better beginning can there be all the world over? A new-comer…remarked, on the simplicity of our arrangements, 'Why! it is nothing to get married here! A few mats and cane-bottomed chairs, and the house is furnished'. And there were many four-roomed cottages thus furnished, where there was as much happiness…as can be found in much more ambitious houses nowadays.

Catherine Spence, 1878

October

MONDAY 8

Labour Day, SA
1847 b. social reformer and suffragette, Rose Scott
1878 b. founding member of the CWA, Ruth Fairfax

TUESDAY 9

Royal National Launceston Show begins
1788 First bridge in Australia built over the Tank Stream in Sydney
1973 Introduction of the $50 note
1974 Introduction of Bankcard

WEDNESDAY 10

1915 Coo-ee March began from Gilgandra, NSW
1986 d. queen of radio serials, Lyndall Barbour

THURSDAY 11

Last quarter of the moon 1.31 pm EST
Launceston Show Day
1852 University of Sydney inaugurated
1953 Sydney *Sun-Herald* first published

FRIDAY 12

1982 Queen Elizabeth II opened the Australian National Gallery in Canberra

SATURDAY 13

Royal National Launceston Show ends

SUNDAY 14

1879 b. writer, Miles Franklin, author of *My Brilliant Career*
1950 b. writer, Kate Grenville, author of *Lilian's Story*

	October					
M	T	W	T	F	S	S
1	2	3	4	5	6	7
8	9	10	11	12	13	14
15	16	17	18	19	20	21
22	23	24	25	26	27	28
29	30	31				

Washing Day

CHOICE OF A DAY FOR WASHING

Washing should be done weekly, as it is unhealthy to allow soiled articles to accumulate.

To lighten labour and to obtain good results, certain preparations should be made the day before.

Tuesday is a suitable day, because preparations can be made on Monday.

Preparation for washing

1 Collect all soiled clothes.
2 Sort into heaps, according to size of wash and variety of articles. No set list can be given which will suit every home.
3 Mend all articles, except socks, stockings and woollen underwear.
4 Remove stains, as ink, fruit, iron rust etc., as the soda in the soap often fixes the stain.
5 Soak all white articles.
6 Prepare the fire under the copper; fill the copper, put the lid on. Have plenty of fuel in readiness.
7 See that all necessary materials are in stock. Make melted soap (soap jelly).
8 Pay special attention to housework and do extra cooking on Monday, so that there will be less to do on Tuesday.

The Common Sense Laundry Book, 1942

THE WASH TUB

...poor dear Charley; he was dreadfully distressed when first we commenced it...then dear old Charley came up to me...looking so distressed and anxious that I could not help exclaiming 'What is the matter Charley?' 'Oh, Charlotte this is a most disgraceful thing is it not?' 'What Charley, having to wash our own clothing?' 'Yes, it appears to me a break up of everything like domestic comfort.' 'Oh, Charley, not at all. Why should it? We shall only have to be very, very busy one day every fortnight...'

...but that same evening poor dear Fanny followed me into my room when I retired...She burst into tears – 'Fanny what is the matter, are you ill?' for I was really frightened at seeing her so distressed. 'Oh no Charlotte, you will say I am very foolish; nothing is the matter but I have such a dread of the washing. I cannot describe to you my horror of it. I hoped such days would never come again but I think they are come upon us now as a punishment for hating the occupation so much. I suppose now I shall never do anything else from Monday morning till Saturday night but stand at the wash tub' and with this speech there came such a torrent of tears that it positively astonished me – however, as well as I could I began to cheer her – told her it was impossible washing her own clothes could employ her a week and that I was quite sure she should be able to do it quite comfortably if she would only look on the bright side and enter into it cheerfully.

Charlotte Bussell, 1842

WASHING A FOX

I have an Arctic fox fur which threatened to cost me a small fortune to keep clean. Warm flour, bran or magnesia were tried in turn without much success. The trouble was to shake all the powder out – all three have a tendency to 'dry' the fur.

At last I took my courage in both hands, whipped up a lather of Lux in a basin of warm water and plunged the stole into it. There followed a panicky moment, for it did look awful – and had cost 20 guineas. However, I had chosen a warm day with a breeze blowing, so I tied my bedraggled fox to the line and stood by shaking and squeezing it until it began to dry. The rest is excellent. No more half-guineas to my expensive furrier who, I am inclined to think, merely *washed* the fur as I did.

Australian Woman's Mirror, October 1926

STOCKINGS

Our legs must be devoid of all shine, and the new sheer grenadine yarn is most flattering. Very open mesh weaves are showing, and may be popular because of their coolness, but there are so few legs that can wear them with success. Some of the new colour creations are dawnette and rose taupe, which are effective with the new blue frockings, but there is a tremendous range of shades, and it is possible to match or contrast any ensemble. Kaffine is a new brown and woodland rose a new pinky beige.

The Home, September 1932

. . .

THE NETHER LIMBS

For centuries, ladies' legs had been shrouded in mystery and many little boys must have grown up thinking they had none. A generation or two before even female feet had been considered a trifle provocative, which accounts for all those saucy shoe and boot vases you see in antique shops. If you have any very early photographs, look at them carefully and you might find some of the female sitters – or rather standers – have a curious floating appearance because many fashionable photographers thought it necessary to erase the feet from the negative. By the time I'm speaking of, however, it was quite respectable for a lady to have feet, even though legs, connected to mysterious regions above, were definitely not approved of and only referred to as 'nether limbs'. Our female friends wore dresses trailing the ground even if arriving by tram.

Eugénie McNeil and Eugénie Crawford, *Ladies Didn't*, 1984

October

MONDAY 15

1810 Australia's first official horse race took place in Hyde Park, Sydney
1903 b. artist, Pixie O'Harris

TUESDAY 16

1863 b. anthropologist, Daisy Bates
1915 b. aviatrix, Nancy-Bird Walton
1970 Westgate Bridge collapsed in Melbourne

WEDNESDAY 17

1854 Melbourne *Age* newspaper founded
1949 Snowy River hydro-electric scheme began

THURSDAY 18

St Luke's Day
1937 Jean Batten took off from Darwin and 5 days and 18 hours later, landed in the UK, setting a new record

FRIDAY 19

New moon 1.37 am EST
1981 d. writer, Dymphna Cusack, author of *Come in Spinner*

SATURDAY 20

1810 Australia's first markets opened in George Street Sydney. The markets later became the Queen Victoria Building
1880 An Act of Parliament changed the name of Hobart Town to Hobart
1973 Sydney Opera House officially opened by Queen Elizabeth II

SUNDAY 21

1895 d. writer and artist, Louisa Meredith, author of *Notes and Sketches of New South Wales*
1908 Dorothea Mackellar's poem 'My Country' published in the *Sydney Mail*

October

M	T	W	T	F	S	S
1	2	3	4	5	6	7
8	9	10	11	12	13	14
15	16	17	18	19	20	21
22	23	24	25	26	27	28
29	30	31				

Tones and semi-tones in color, running the entire scale of today's color requirements for smart dress, are to be had in rich array in this remarkable "over-knees" silk stocking.

PHOENIX HOSIERY
WHOLESALE: FRANKLIN P. BOLT, BATHURST HOUSE, BATHURST-CASTLEREAGH STS., SYDNEY

The Scorpio Birthday
23 OCTOBER – 21 NOVEMBER

The symbol for Scorpio is a Scorpion, or Eagle, but the usual one is the Scorpion. Scorpio rules the sex functions and the eliminative functions of the body. Scorpio corresponds to the eighth sign of the Zodiac, which rules death, dreams, sleep, wills and legacies. Scorpios are easy for an astrologer to pick out because of their usually dark eyes, which have the 'look of the eagle,' an intense gaze, unlike any other in the birthday circle.

Scorpio complaints are usually associated with the parts of the body already mentioned, but they are so strongly vital that they are seldom ill. They like to live near water, or near orchards.

The Scorpio word is 'Well!' the motto 'Read the Secrets of Nature.'

Aspro Year Book, 1936

ROSES EVERYWHERE

Rose-tinted spectacles have long been a figure of speech, but spectacles which are actually rose-coloured are now becoming increasingly popular. It is claimed for this new optical glass that it absorbs an excess of light, which might, otherwise, harm the sight. The tints are in three strengths, the lightest rose colour being almost invisible. So no one needs yearn for the proverbial 'rose-coloured spectacles'; the optician is only too willing to supply his customers with them.

Helen's Weekly, September 1927

October

MONDAY 22

TUESDAY 23

1810 b. 'factory' matron, Mary Hutchinson (the factory was the female house of correction)

WEDNESDAY 24

United Nations Day
Royal Hobart Show begins
1980 Multicultural television stations launched in Australia

THURSDAY 25

Hobart Show Day
1942 b. singer, Helen Reddy
1961 Australian Medical Association registered in Canberra

FRIDAY 26

First quarter of the moon 6.26 am EST

SATURDAY 27

Royal Hobart Show ends
1889 b. swimmer, Fanny Durack

SUNDAY 28

Daylight saving begins NSW, SA and Vic.
1774 Norfolk Island named by Captain Cook after the Duke of Norfolk

October

M	T	W	T	F	S	S
1	2	3	4	5	6	7
8	9	10	11	12	13	14
15	16	17	18	19	20	21
22	23	24	25	26	27	28
29	30	31				

Leaves from a November Notebook

Our clime is heavenly, and while you are burning the front breadth of your frock and the nebs of your shoes at an excellent fire of Newcastle coals, I am sitting in the Verandah surrounded by my little flower garden of British, Cape and Australian flowers pouring forth their odour (for the large white lily is now in bloom) and a variety of beautiful little birds most brilliant in plumage sporting around me. These little creatures seem quite delighted at the acquisition they have made in our emigration and are much tamer than any but the robin and sparrow in England. There is a small bird called the Australian robin with shining black back and head, and the breast of a very bright scarlet. Also a little bird of a complete blue colour all over resembling Smalt or Cobalt, with short green wings, and the Honeyeater are minutely beautiful. I cannot describe them – they have a long curved beak which they insert into the cup of the different flowers and the symmetry of their form is perfect, it accords with the elegance of their food.

Georgiana Molloy, 1832

TO CURE WARTS

Take a piece of raw beef steeped in vinegar for twenty-four hours, tie it on the part affected. Apply each night for two weeks.

Australian Etiquette, 1885

October ✒ November

MONDAY 29

1825 b. soprano, Catherine Hayes
1872 b. founding member of the National Council of Women, Dr Edith Barrett

TUESDAY 30

WEDNESDAY 31

Hallowe'en
1825 b. writer and feminist, Catherine Spence, author of *Clara Morrison*

THURSDAY 1

All Saints' Day
1838 World's first stamped envelopes issued in Sydney
1860 b. explorer and diarist, Emily Caroline Creaghe

FRIDAY 2

All Souls' Day
1788 Parramatta became second settlement on Australia's mainland
1834 b. superintendent of Marsden Training Home, Eliza Hassall

SATURDAY 3

Full moon 7.48 am EST
1897 b. theatrical producer, Doris Fitton
1920 b. poet, Kath Walker

SUNDAY 4

1939 d. writer, Amy Mack, author of *A Bush Calendar*, and editor of the women's page of The *Sydney Morning Herald*

	November					
M	T	W	T	F	S	S
			1	2	3	4
5	6	7	8	9	10	11
12	13	14	15	16	17	18
19	20	21	22	23	24	25
26	27	28	29	30		

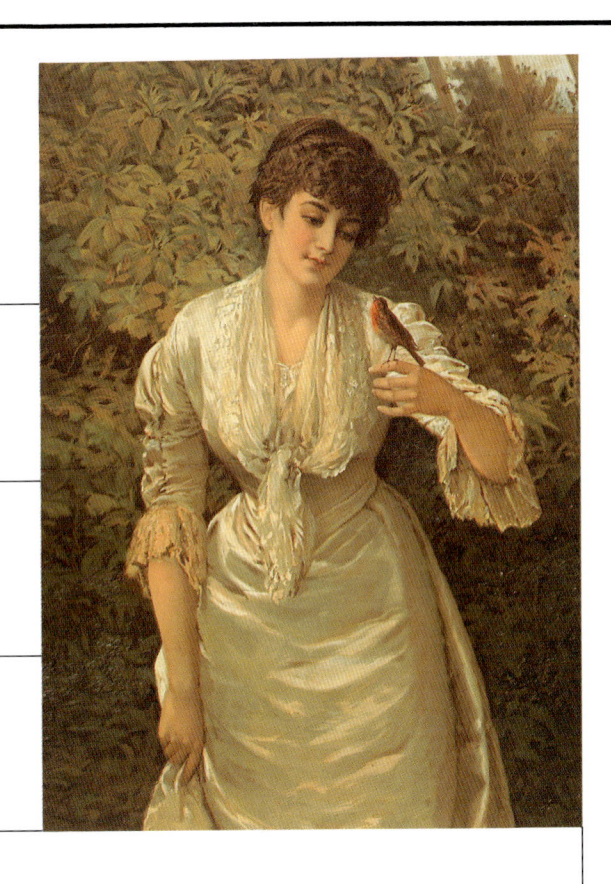

A CUP NOW AND THEN

Looking back, we learn that the inaugural Melbourne Cup meeting was held in 1861, with a purse of '20 sovs., 10 sovs. forfeit, or 5 sovs. if declared, with 200 sovs. added by the Victorian Turf Club' to quote a race record of that day.

In all, the winner collected £610. This race was run over the two mile course at Flemington and was won by Archer, owned by a New South Welshman. The 5-year-old, carrying 9st. 7lb., won in 3 min. 52 sec. This horse, the finest of its day, also won the next Melbourne Cup, carrying the punishing weight of 10st. 2lb.

In a few years the Melbourne Cup came to be considered the test for the foremost Australasian horses where, as an older writer has it, 'the best horses of every Colony should try their mettle'...

An estimate of the total number of persons present at the first Melbourne Cup, boastfully places the number at 4,000. Last year the attendance approximated 120,000!...

By the way – do you know what was said about us as recently as 1907? 'Although the prizes offered are valuable enough, there is a rough and ready way about colonial racing which would not commend itself to "drawing-room" sportsmen'! Now the question which is worrying me is this – Have we advanced or have "drawing-room" sportsmen deteriorated?

Helen's Weekly, November 1927

November

MONDAY 5

Recreation Day, northern Tas.
1956 ABC's television service opened

TUESDAY 6

Melbourne Cup Day
1913 b. Una Prentice, first woman law graduate to be admitted to the Ql
1975 d. swimmer and film star, Annette Kellerman

WEDNESDAY 7

1861 Melbourne Cup first held and won by Archer
1926 b. opera singer, Dame Joan Sutherland
1930 Phar Lap won the Melbourne Cup

THURSDAY 8

FRIDAY 9

Last quarter of the moon 11.02 pm EST
1793 b. charity organiser, Fanny Macleay

SATURDAY 10

1825 City of Brisbane named

SUNDAY 11

Remembrance Day
1903 b. actress, Queenie Ashton
1941 Australian War Memorial opened in Canberra
1975 Whitlam government dismissed

November

M	T	W	T	F	S	S
			1	2	3	4
5	6	7	8	9	10	11
12	13	14	15	16	17	18
19	20	21	22	23	24	25
26	27	28	29	30		

THE CHIC WOMAN TRAVELS

The clangour of the ship's gong gives warning of the imminent departure. Soon the last streamer breaks, and the lines move off down the harbour. The thoughts of the passengers inevitably veer from those they have left behind on the wharf to the new experiences that await them. For the women passengers much of their enjoyment will depend on how they have dealt with the question of clothes and luggage.

In regard to the latter, conditions have changed greatly in the last few years. When the smart Sydney woman sets off on her travels she is no longer satisfied merely to have her clothes correct and charming. Her luggage also must measure up to the same standard of perfection. Nowadays a chic voyageuse – whether hailing from Paris or Sydney – has trim new luggage as spruce in appearance as her charming self.

One of the newest conceits is to have coloured luggage, and some of the new suit cases and hat boxes are striking studies in scarlet or bright blue. One advantage that is claimed for them is that they can be easily picked out from among an assorted heap of other people's impedimenta. Less conspicuous, and in better taste, are suit cases and hat boxes in shiny black, piped narrowly in red or blue, or plain navy blue and grey leather boxes.

The Home, April 1928

November

MONDAY 12

1938 b. writer, Sarah Dowse

TUESDAY 13

1846 Colony of North Australia proclaimed
1984 111 women demonstrators arrested, protesting against US bases at Pine Gap

WEDNESDAY 14

1836 b. Aboriginal leader, Louisa Briggs

THURSDAY 15

FRIDAY 16

1920 Queensland and Northern Territory Aerial Services Ltd (Qantas) founded

SATURDAY 17

New moon 7.05 pm EST
1831 b. artist, Adelaide Ironside
1869 Suez Canal opened, shortening sea voyage between England and Australia

SUNDAY 18

1907 b. writer, Gwen Meredith, author of *Blue Hills*
1986 Queen Victoria Building re-opened in Sydney

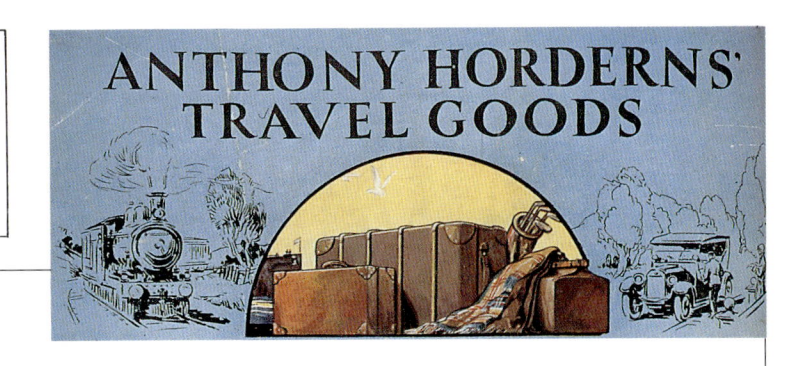

November

M	T	W	T	F	S	S
			1	2	3	4
5	6	7	8	9	10	11
12	13	14	15	16	17	18
19	20	21	22	23	24	25
26	27	28	29	30		

ANTHONY HORDERNS' TRAVEL GOODS

The Romance of Travel

Going to the Ball

One hundred years ago, going to a ball was a great occasion. It offered young people the opportunity to meet eligible members of the opposite sex – and for mothers a chance to get marriageable daughters off their hands. The ball in Australia, as in Europe, was an event governed by strict laws of etiquette – or supposedly, anyway!

THE SHILLING BALL

[The 'shilling ball'] is not only 'quite colonial' but, I imagine, quite peculiar, also. The entrance to the festive scene had a curtain drawn across, which the visitors passed, after paying the introductory shilling, and found themselves in a very large, clean, well-proportioned room, brilliantly lighted, and with an excellent band playing good modern dance music. Plenty of comfortable seats were ranged round the room, and a master of the ceremonies paraded to and fro. Cards of the ensuing dances were hung up, and all conducted, *salon les règles*. And the company! No gauzes, laces, tarlatans, nor satin shoes – and right little superfine broadcloth decked that singular assembly. The room was filled with men and women of the working classes, in their every-day dresses, men in fustian coats, blue and red, and serge shirts, divers sorts of frocks and 'pimpers', and the commonest cord or fustian trousers, trade-grimed or mud-bespattered; all with their hats on, and the majority with pipe or cigar in their mouths. The women, young and older, in dowdy common gowns, shawls, bonnets, and walking shoes. These people, in the most correct and orderly manner imaginable, were dancing quadrilles, polkas, waltzes etc...Not a shadow of impropriety or indecorum was visible.

Louisa Meredith, Melbourne, 1856

BALL DRESS

Ball dressing requires less art than the nice gradations of costume in the dinner dress, and the dress for evening parties. For a ball, everything should be light and diaphanous, somewhat fanciful and airy. The heavy, richly-trimmed silk is only appropriate to those who do not dance. The richest velvets, the brightest and most delicate tints in silk, the most expensive laces, elaborate coiffures, a large display of diamonds, artificial flowers for the head-dress and natural flowers for hand bouquets, all belong, more or less, to the costume for a large ball.

Australian Etiquette, 1885

SUPPER

The supper-room at a ball is thrown open generally at twelve o'clock. The table is made as elegant as beautiful china, cut glass and an abundance of flowers can make it. The hot dishes are oysters, stewed, fried, broiled and scalloped, chicken, game, etc., and the cold dishes are such as boned turkey, *boeuf à la mode*, chicken salad, lobster salad and raw oysters. When supper is announced, the host leads the way with the lady to whom he wishes to show especial attention, who may be an elderly lady, or a stranger or a bride. The hostess remains until the last, with the gentleman who takes her to supper, unless some distinguished guest is present, with whom she leads the way.

Australian Etiquette, 1885

WHAT A DISASTER!

My third dance was at the Royal Military College, Duntroon, in its early years.

After a hot dusty day at the sports, I found when I unpacked at the doctor's house where I was billeted for the night, that I had not brought any stockings with me. I had been wearing thick, white, ribbed silk, knitted (by me) stockings, the last word when worn with brogues but unwearable with satin evening shoes. What a disaster! Mrs Doctor could not help me, as she only wore black cotton stockings. I suggested I could go to the dance barelegged and she was adamant I could do no such thing. So, hoping Elma Rutledge could help me I set off in my white satin dress, bought for the Prince of Wales dance at Rona, and brogues along a dusty lane lined with flowering hawthorn hedgerows past the Parade Ground to B Quarters, where Elma was staying with old friends. She was able to lend me a pair of white silk stockings so I could attend the dance not as a figure of fun as I feared, or in disgrace as Mrs Doctor feared. 'I could have danced all night' and did.

Helen Rutledge, *My Grandfather's House*, 1986

The Sagittarius Birthday
22 NOVEMBER – 21 DECEMBER

The symbol for Sagittarius is the Centaur, half man, half horse.

Sagittarius rules the hips and thighs, and corresponds to the ninth house in the horoscope, which stands for religion, philosophy, law, and travel.

You can pick Sagittarians by their strong teeth, oval faces, ruddy or sunburnt skins, hair with chestnut lights in it (in youth, at least), well-marked eyebrows, prominent noses, restless ways, enthusiasm, habit of wearing their garments open at the neck, and by the slight stammer or occasional halting impediment in the speech.

The typical ailments are bronchitis, poor digestion, and blood disorders. The cure, plenty of rest, fresh air, and cheerful surroundings.

The Sagittarius word is 'If,' the motto 'Inspiration.' Your type loves the hills and upper rooms, warmth, fires, sunshine, and plenty of fresh air.

Aspro Year Book, 1936

TREACHEROUS TAFFETA

For evening wear there is quite a big choice of fabrics that come up smiling after a sojourn in a trunk. Lace frocks are specially useful. Better still is a frock of the new crepe chiffon, with long lace sleeves. Chenille georgette is another useful fabric in this connection, and beaded frocks are also perfect for packing. The one fabric that must be eschewed is the treacherous taffeta, as it has a disconcerting habit of falling to pieces in the tropics.

The Home, April 1928

November

MONDAY 19
1919 b. Margaret Whitlam
1939 *Sunday Telegraph* first published in Sydney

TUESDAY 20
1897 b. composer, Margaret Sutherland
1897 b. aviatrix, Lores Bonney
1947 Princess Elizabeth (now Queen Elizabeth II) married the Duke of Edinburgh

WEDNESDAY 21
Presentation of the Blessed Virgin Mary
1886 b. novelist and poet, Ada Cambridge, author of *A Marked Man*
1912 b. concert pianist, Eileen Joyce

THURSDAY 22
1956 XVI Olympiad held in Melbourne – Australia won 13 gold, 8 silver and 4 bronze medals

FRIDAY 23
1956 b. swimmer, Shane Gould. Between April 1971 and January 1972 Gould held the world record for every women's freestyle event

SATURDAY 24
1642 Abel Tasman sighted Tas.
1816 b. diarist, Annie Dawbin
1873 b. poet, Dora Wilcox

SUNDAY 25
First quarter of the moon 11.11 pm EST
Feast of Christ the King
Tasmania Day

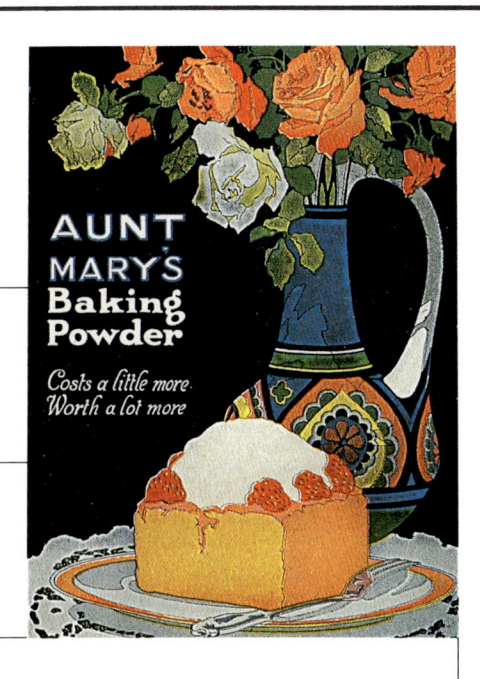

		November				
M	T	W	T	F	S	S
		1	2	3	4
5	6	7	8	9	10	11
12	13	14	15	16	17	18
19	20	21	22	23	24	25
26	27	28	29	30		

AUNT MARY'S Baking Powder

Costs a little more. Worth a lot more

Visit SOUTH AUSTRALIA for your next Holiday

SEE ADELAIDE, "the City Beautiful," the SOUTH EAST with its Crater Lakes, rugged Coast line, and the far-famed NARACOORTE CAVES, the picturesque SOUTH COAST, the fruitful MURRAY VALLEY and other well known pleasure resorts.

Motor Excursions through the MOUNT LOFTY RANGES daily.

Trips by RAIL, ROAD and RIVER through MOUNTAIN, VALLEY and PLAIN.

Through bookings at Excursion rates from SYDNEY and MELBOURNE.

PICCADILLY FROM "CARMINOW," MT. LOFTY (visited by Tourist Bureau Charabanc)

For further information apply to the GOVT. TOURIST BUREAU in each State, or direct to the
GOVERNMENT INTELLIGENCE AND TOURIST BUREAU
KING WILLIAM STREET, ADELAIDE   Victor H. Ryan, Director

Leaves from a December Notebook

We make pleasant raids into the new garden every afternoon. The first ripe figs were gathered on the 6th, but now there are Chinese peaches and mulberries, as well as quantities of figs. I cannot say I like the flavour of these double blossomed peaches. The Moreton Bay chestnut is now in flower, of a scarlet and yellow colour, and grows in clusters on the bare branches without leaves near them.

Annabella Boswell, 1843

SUMMER

The bloom of spring is short lived. The first hot north winds of summer sweep the green before them and the countryside turns to the colours of sand and bone, lit here and there by the crimson and rose tassels of flowering gum trees. The solid imported trees soon look stale and tattered and their colour changes before its time. One is reminded of the sparse lacey shade of the eucalypts, their leaves turned cunningly edgeways to the sun.

Maie Casey, *An Australian Story 1837-1907*, 1962

November December

MONDAY 26

1952 b. tennis player, Wendy Turnbull

TUESDAY 27

1889 Miss Mary Anne Harris, daughter of the Lord Mayor, opened the Great Hall of the Sydney Town Hall
1969 d. May Gibbs, author of *Snugglepot and Cuddlepie*

WEDNESDAY 28

1886 b. community worker and politician, Margaret McIntyre
1932 Dog on the Tuckerbox statue unveiled outside Gundagai, as a monument to pioneers of the area
1948 The first Holden ('Australia's Own Car') went on sale for £760

THURSDAY 29

1934 Eighteen people died in Vic. when the Yarra River broke its banks

FRIDAY 30

St Andrew's Day
Devonport Show Day, Tas.
1878 'Advance Australia Fair' first performed
1952 d. nurse, Sister Elizabeth Kenny

SATURDAY 1

First day of summer
1892 b. composer, Mirrie Hill
1915 SA Women's Police Force established

SUNDAY 2

Full moon 5.50 pm EST
Advent Sunday
1876 Grace Bussell rescued crew and forty-eight passengers of the *Georgette* – a steamer wrecked off the WA coast

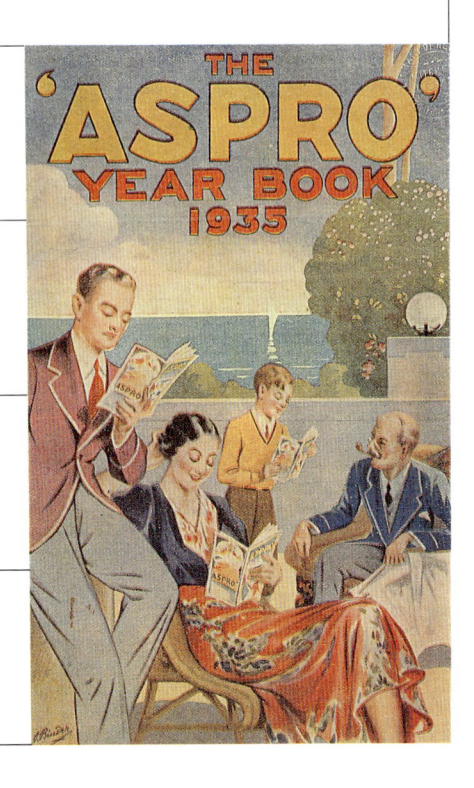

November

M	T	W	T	F	S	S
		1	2	3	4
5	6	7	8	9	10	11
12	13	14	15	16	17	18
19	20	21	22	23	24	25
26	27	28	29	30

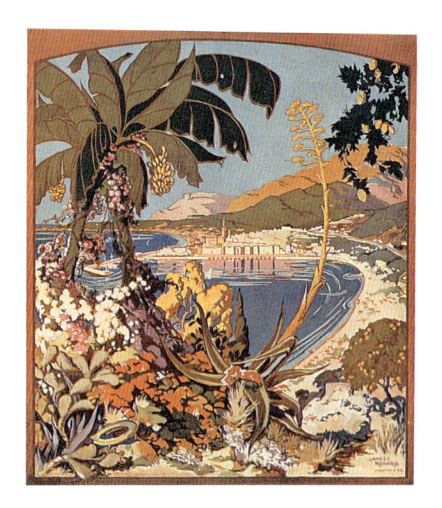

ALLIGATOR!

Between the root of the tree and bank there was now a great gap where the tide was rushing through with tremendous force, and close along side of me there rose something that, for the moment, I thought was another half-sunken tree. Then it fell, a gray, loathsome creature that almost paralyzed me with fear as I marked the long line of its greedy-looking jaws. I knew that the river teemed with alligators, but, somehow or other, I had never given it a thought. Its horny back was not more than a foot below me, and I hardly dared to breathe, much less to move. It slid along the log and I felt the vibration of its body rubbing as it came up on the other side…Uncertain as to its movements, it sluggishly played round and round. My eyes were riveted on it, and in the horror of the moment I forgot the river, tide, and everything else, as with the rising water it came so close again that my feet almost touched as it stirred the slimy ooze and mud from the bank with its tail…Now, as if waiting for the supreme moment, its opportunity to spring, it rose the full length of its body and menacingly clashed its jaws, then with snout down stream, it went under, leaving nothing in its wake but a long ripple on the surface of the water.

Ellis Rowan, *A Flower Hunter in Queensland and New Zealand*, 1898

December

MONDAY 3

1825 Tas. declared a separate state from NSW
1884 b. Australia's first policewoman, Lillian Armfield
1962 d. poet, Dame Mary Gilmore

TUESDAY 4

1791 b. philanthropist, Lady Jane Franklin
1856 b. doctor and feminist, Constance Stone
1883 b. writer, Katherine Susannah Prichard, author of *Coonardoo*

WEDNESDAY 5

THURSDAY 6

St Nicholas' Day

FRIDAY 7

1926 b. writer, Amirah Inglis, author of *An Un-Australian Childhood*

SATURDAY 8

Immaculate Conception of the Blessed Virgin Mary
1919 b. artist, Jacqueline Hick
1987 Melbourne's Queen Street massacre

SUNDAY 9

Last quarter of the moon 12.04 pm EST

December						
M	T	W	T	F	S	S
31					1	2
3	4	5	6	7	8	9
10	11	12	13	14	15	16
17	18	19	20	21	22	23
24	25	26	27	28	29	30

Ellis Rowan

December

TAKING TENNIS SERIOUSLY

Have you noticed in small suburban clubs how many women go down to the court on Saturdays and Sundays merely to talk? To them it is only a meeting-place where they see some of their friends once a week and, accordingly, they make the most of it, having a lively gossip, a thorough exchange of news and a good laugh...

Quite a lot of women, odd though it sounds, seem to think they will lose their personality and charm if they fail to laugh and joke on the court, and try instead to play properly and well. They have the idea that they will become 'too serious, too dull, too mannish' – and lose their feminine charm. And loss of 'feminine charm,' of course, in their minds, connotes loss of interest on the part of the males of the species.

This is quite a false idea, and the woman who devotes herself systematically to improving her game will soon find it out. She will discover that she...has gained the admiration and respect of the male members of her club...

You become popular. You are invited to play at various places by people who like a good game. There is always something 'on' – you are always in demand.

Australian Woman's Mirror, December 1926

MONDAY 10

1859 Qld declared a separate state from NSW
1882 First strike by a group of women at a Melbourne clothing factory

TUESDAY 11

1873 b. blind writer and teacher, Tilly Aston
1936 b. fashion promoter and media personality, Maggie Tabberer

WEDNESDAY 12

THURSDAY 13

1890 b. bohemian and writer, Dulcie Deamer
1955 Edna Everage's stage début

FRIDAY 14

1878 Horse-drawn trams first appeared on Adelaide's streets
1908 Bill passed establishing ACT

SATURDAY 15

1882 First all-woman union formed (Tailoresses' Union)
1904 b. feminist, Edna Ryan

SUNDAY 16

1898 Australia's first women's bowling club founded in Melbourne
1899 WA Government introduced female suffrage
1903 Australian women voted for the first time at a Federal election

		December				
M	T	W	T	F	S	S
31					1	2
3	4	5	6	7	8	9
10	11	12	13	14	15	16
17	18	19	20	21	22	23
24	25	26	27	28	29	30

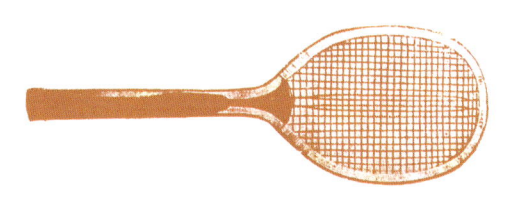

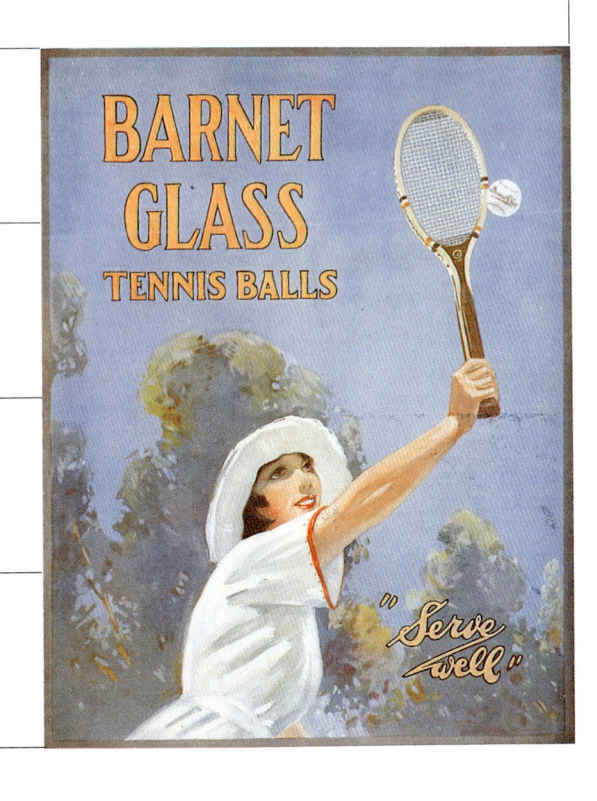

December

CHRISTMAS PRESENT – AND FUTURE

24 December 1892. Lil, Rose, Rex and I went to town and shopped all day. Between us we got Mother a lovely little gold brooch, a silver bread fork and I got her too a new screen of pleated art muslin for drawing room. For Mr Cope we got a Canary Breeding Cage and a silk handkerchief. For Lil I got a bottle of scent and a serge skirt. For Rose a lace cap and 1/- Rex 1/6. Louie a scent bottle, etc. etc. My Xmas presents were, from Mr Cope 8 collars and a silk handkerchief. Mother a writing case and nailbrush, Lil *Everybody's Book of Poems* and from H., Carrol's *Through the Looking Glass*. He says *The Bulletin* editor says my story 'The Little Duchess' is good and accepted, he is going to write to me. My first thing in *The Bulletin*! I believe I shall be successful in the literary line after all. I *will* be.

Philippa Poole (ed.), *The Diaries of Ethel Turner*, 1979

MONDAY 17
New moon 2.22 pm EST
1863 Great Flood in Melbourne
1945 b. Channel swimmer, Linda McGill
1967 Harold Holt drowned

TUESDAY 18
1841 First Australian children's book, *A Mother's Offering to her Children*, published in Sydney
1874 b. writer, G. B. Lancaster (Edith Joan Lyttleton), author of *Pageant*
1950 b. film director, Gillian Armstrong

WEDNESDAY 19
1972 Last Australian troops left Vietnam

THURSDAY 20
1915 Evacuation of Gallipoli
1984 d. artist, Grace Cossington-Smith

FRIDAY 21
1881 b. headmistress, Winifred West
1894 SA became first state to give women the right to vote and to stand for parliament
1925 d. producer and Australia's first film star, Lottie Lyell, aged only 35

SATURDAY 22
Shortest day
Summer solstice 1.07 pm EST

SUNDAY 23
1885 Art Gallery of NSW officially opened
1891 b. artist, Dorrit Black
1946 East West Airlines formed
1984 d. writer, Joan Lindsay, author of *Picnic at Hanging Rock*

December

M	T	W	T	F	S	S
31					1	2
3	4	5	6	7	8	9
10	11	12	13	14	15	16
17	18	19	20	21	22	23
24	25	26	27	28	29	30

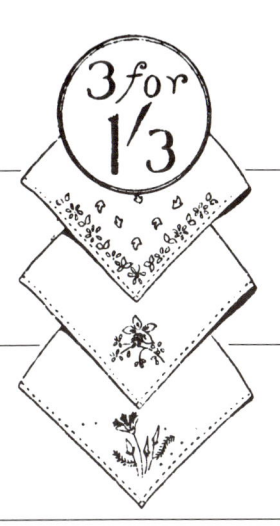

Christmas

PLUM PUDDING AND PARROT PIE

December 25th 1836. This being Christmas Day and Sunday, Divine Service was held for the first time in the rush hut of the principal Surveyor a short distance from our Tents. We attended, taking our seats with us, the signal for assembling being the firing of a gun...the thermometer standing at a 100...In the afternoon we took a walk around the Lagoon and saw a large Ghuana basking in the sun, it was about three feet long, in form like a Lizard with a long pointed tail...We kept up the old custom of Christmas as far as having a plum pudding for dinner, likewise a Ham and a Parrot Pie, but one of our neighbours had a large piece of roast Beef.

From the *Diary of Mary Thomas*

QUIET HAPPINESS

Monday 25th Christmas Day Received a handsome 'Christmas Box' from James in the shape of a black watered silk dress, some handkerchiefs & a shawl trim. Stewart also gave me two prs of gloves. Reading & strolling about till twelve when we had Prayers – dined on Roast beef & plum pudding at two o'clock. Lying on the sofa, Stewart reading aloud to us; in the afternoon as soon as it became cool & pleasant we drove to the Lake & had tea there, picking up shells on Haslam's Beach while it was preparing – returned home at dusk, offered up our evening sacrifice with grateful & overflowing hearts & when the children were in bed & the house quiet we went into the Office & spent the hours till bed time in quiet happiness. N.E.

Mary Braidwood Mowle, *The Life and Times of a Colonial Woman*, 1854

CHRISTMAS CHEER

Already a green shoot spread across the paddocks, as though a paint brush had been drawn lightly across brown parchment...On that same day there came a large case of 'Christmas cheer', a gesture of good will from our company. There were a dozen bottles of lager, which I quickly annexed for the Christmas dinner-table, some sherry and wine for me, and a bottle each of Scotch and rum for Danny.

...There was also an interesting box filled with such items as asparagus, nuts, olives, a huge tin of chocolates, two tins of biscuits, and tinned plum pudding. As neither Pete nor I could make plum pudding, this was certainly a windfall.

Christmas Eve was humid and still, with the usual long dark cloud sulking on the horizon. In a truly feudal manner we invited the black staff to the pantry after supper and issued them each with a half pannikin of sherry.

Elizabeth O'Connor, *Steak for Breakfast,* 1958

The Capricorn Birthday
22 DECEMBER – 19 JANUARY

The symbol for Capricorn is the Goat, and this sign rules the knees in the human body. Capricorn corresponds to the tenth house in the horoscope, which rules business and social standing in the community.

The Capricorn natives are easy to pick and fall into two main groups. The first is the boney, 'dour,' lantern-jawed type, with a thick neck, and face, brow bones prominent, thin, wiry form, weak chest development, sloping shoulders, and angular movements, appearing as though they would fall to pieces at any moment. The other is perhaps the handsomest type in the whole birthday circle – dark-eyed, swarthy, Spanish-looking, grave and serious, but fascinating in the extreme. Most Capricorns walk rather badly, and are inclined to be knock-kneed, and all of them tend to delicacy in childhood, improved vitality in adulthood, and leather toughness in old age.

The Capricorn word is 'But' and the motto 'Excelsior!' They are very shrewd; you simply can't 'kid' a Capricorn!

Aspro Year Book, 1936

SQUINT-EYES AND CROSS-EYES

Parents should also be careful that their children do not become squint or cross-eyed through any carelessness. A child's hair hanging down loosely over its eyes, or a bonnet projecting too far over them, or a loose ribbon or tape fluttering over the forehead, is sometimes sufficient to direct the sight irregularly until it becomes permanently crossed.

Australian Etiquette, 1885

December

MONDAY 24

Christmas Eve
1873 b. artist and feminist, Portia Geach
1956 *Woman's Day* first published

TUESDAY 25

Christmas Day
First quarter of the moon 1.16 pm EST
1859 Rabbits first released in Australia, as game
1957 First Australian Christmas stamps issued

WEDNESDAY 26

Boxing Day
St Stephen's Day
1906 Australia's first full-length feature film produced – *The Story of the Kelly Gang*

THURSDAY 27

St John's Day

FRIDAY 28

Holy Innocents' Day
Proclamation Day, SA
1836 SA became a separate colony
1857 b. headmistress, Eliza Fewings

SATURDAY 29

St Thomas a Becket's Day
The Holy Family's Day
1879 b. Australia's first woman architect, Florence Taylor
1912 b. composer, Peggy Glanville Hicks

SUNDAY 30

1921 b. sports administrator, Patricia Bridges

		December				
M	T	W	T	F	S	S
31					1	2
3	4	5	6	7	8	9
10	11	12	13	14	15	16
17	18	19	20	21	22	23
24	25	26	27	28	29	30

December / January

MONDAY 31	
New Year's Eve (holiday NSW)	
TUESDAY 1	
New Year's Day	
WEDNESDAY 2	
THURSDAY 3	
FRIDAY 4	
SATURDAY 5	
SUNDAY 6	

NASTY, CREEPY THINGS!

How the gentlemen would laugh at me! I lay there thinking of all my blunders. I was always being chaffed for something or other. Only two Sundays before I had been lying on the terrace, outside the dining-room reading. The tea bell rang. I made to get up, and felt four legs clawing at me and a long tail wrapping round. I clutched the thing round the neck and screamed the place down. Everybody rushed to see what was the matter, but I would not let any one come near me till one of the chaplains got behind me, held my arms, and the horrid creature fell down. It had got up between my skirt and my foundation. It was a frilled lizard, four inches across the back and ten inches long, a brownish green, all foaming at the mouth. They killed it even though it was harmless and they chipped me.

There was plenty of nasty, creepy things to put up with, and swarms of little green frogs. They called them Queensland canaries. When I laid the supper the next Sunday one flopped down off the fanlight. I got the broom, but could not find it. After I carried in the supper, the bell rang. I was not supposed to answer. However, Mrs Lavender did not come and it rang again, so I went. The cheese dish stood on the corner of the table with half a Stilton on it.

'Will you please take it away?' said Mr Power.

I picked up the dish, looked in the cheese, and there sat the frog! The dish went one way, the frog another, the cheese a third, and I tore out of the room.

A Girl at Government House, 1932

		January				
M	T	W	T	F	S	S
		1	2	3	4	5	6
7	8	9	10	11	12	13
14	15	16	17	18	19	20
21	22	23	24	25	26	27
28	29	30	31			

Children's game board, *c.* 1890

School Holidays

Listed below are the dates for school holidays across Australia

NEW SOUTH WALES
18 December 1989–26 January 1990
 (Eastern Division)
18 December 1989–2 February 1990
 (Western Division)
13 April 1990–20 April 1990
 2 July 1990–13 July 1990
24 September 1990–5 October 1990
17 December 1990–28 January 1991
 (Eastern Division)
17 December 1990–4 February 1991
 (Western Division)

VICTORIA
23 December 1989–6 February 1990
13 April 1990–20 April 1990
 2 July 1990–13 July 1990
24 September 1990–5 October 1990
24 December 1990–(not available)

QUEENSLAND
16 December 1989–28 January 1990
13 April 1990–20 April 1990
18 June 1990–29 June 1990
17 September 1990–28 September 1990
17 December 1990–28 January 1991

SOUTH AUSTRALIA
18 December 1989–29 January 1990
13 April 1990–20 April 1990
 2 July 1990–13 July 1990
24 September 1990–8 October 1990
17 December 1990–(not available)

WESTERN AUSTRALIA
21 December 1989–29 January 1990
13 April 1990–27 April 1990
 9 July 1990–23 July 1990
1 October–12 October 1990
20 December 1990–(not available)

TASMANIA
21 December 1989–19 February 1990
28 May 1990–8 June 1990
 3 September 1990–14 September 1990
21 December 1990–(not available)

NORTHERN TERRITORY
18 December 1989–26 January 1990
 9 April 1990–16 April 1990
25 June 1990–20 July 1990
30 September 1990–4 October 1990
17 December 1990–(not available)

AUSTRALIAN CAPITAL TERRITORY
18 December 1989–26 January 1990
13 April 1990–20 April 1990
 2 July 1990–13 July 1990
24 September 1990–5 October 1990
17 December 1990– (not available)

Family Birthdays 1990

Person	How old this year	Date of Birth

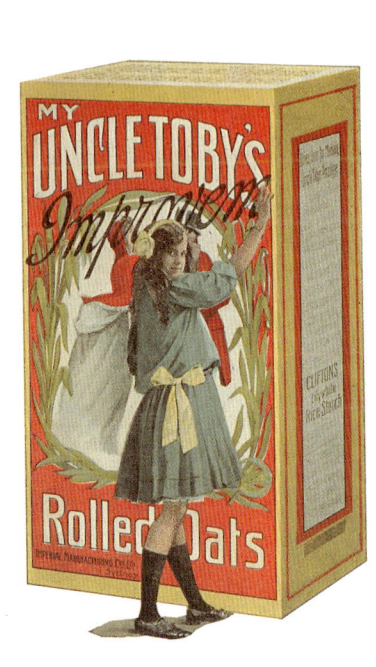

Family Photograph Album

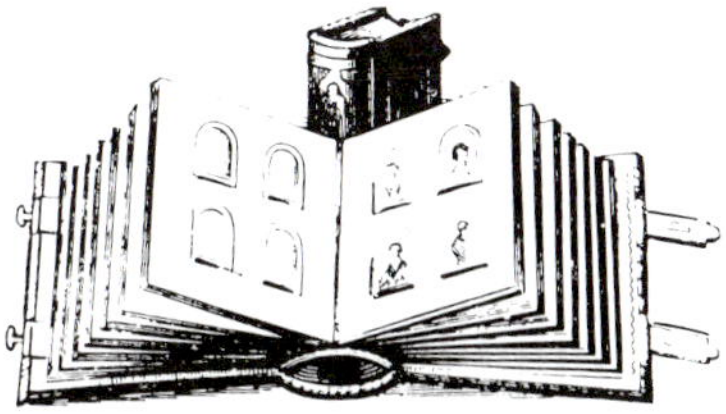

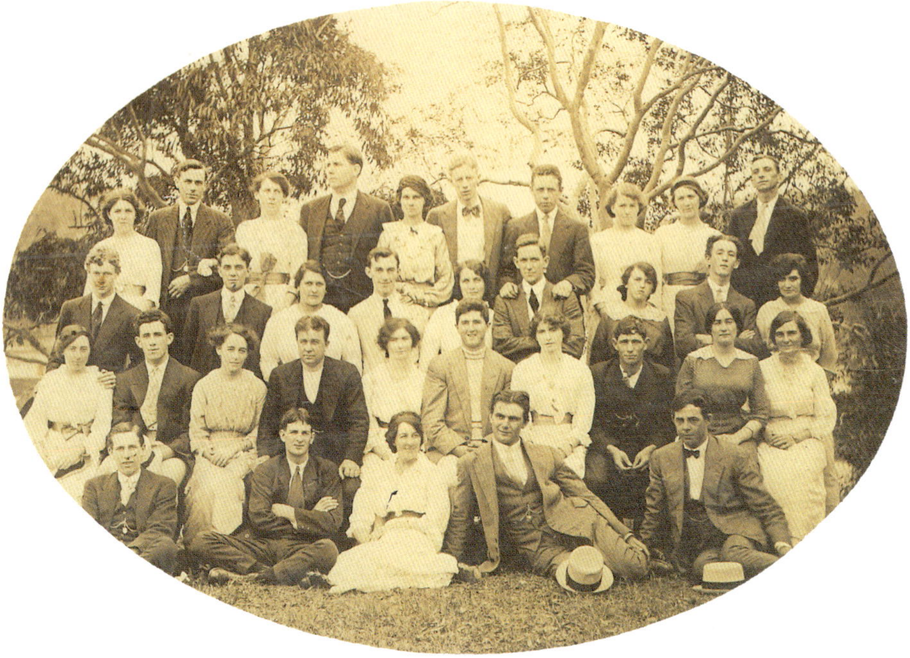

Notes

1990

1991

Visitors to Our Home

Guest　　　　　　　　　Date　　　　　　　　　Comments

WELCOME

Guest　　　　　　　　Date　　　　　　　　　　Comments

Addresses and Telephone Numbers

Name and Address | Telephone

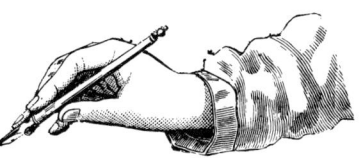

Name and Address   Telephone

Addresses and Telephone Numbers

Name and Address	Telephone

1989

January
M	T	W	T	F	S	S
30	31					1
2	3	4	5	6	7	8
9	10	11	12	13	14	15
16	17	18	19	20	21	22
23	24	25	26	27	28	29

February
M	T	W	T	F	S	S
		1	2	3	4	5
6	7	8	9	10	11	12
13	14	15	16	17	18	19
20	21	22	23	24	25	26
27	28					

March
M	T	W	T	F	S	S
		1	2	3	4	5
6	7	8	9	10	11	12
13	14	15	16	17	18	19
20	21	22	23	24	25	26
27	28	29	30	31		

April
M	T	W	T	F	S	S
					1	2
3	4	5	6	7	8	9
10	11	12	13	14	15	16
17	18	19	20	21	22	23
24	25	26	27	28	29	30

May
M	T	W	T	F	S	S
1	2	3	4	5	6	7
8	9	10	11	12	13	14
15	16	17	18	19	20	21
22	23	24	25	26	27	28
29	30	31				

June
M	T	W	T	F	S	S
			1	2	3	4
5	6	7	8	9	10	11
12	13	14	15	16	17	18
19	20	21	22	23	24	25
26	27	28	29	30		

July
M	T	W	T	F	S	S
31					1	2
3	4	5	6	7	8	9
10	11	12	13	14	15	16
17	18	19	20	21	22	23
24	25	26	27	28	29	30

August
M	T	W	T	F	S	S
	1	2	3	4	5	6
7	8	9	10	11	12	13
14	15	16	17	18	19	20
21	22	23	24	25	26	27
28	29	30	31			

September
M	T	W	T	F	S	S
				1	2	3
4	5	6	7	8	9	10
11	12	13	14	15	16	17
18	19	20	21	22	23	24
25	26	27	28	29	30	

October
M	T	W	T	F	S	S
30	31					1
2	3	4	5	6	7	8
9	10	11	12	13	14	15
16	17	18	19	20	21	22
23	24	25	26	27	28	29

November
M	T	W	T	F	S	S
		1	2	3	4	5
6	7	8	9	10	11	12
13	14	15	16	17	18	19
20	21	22	23	24	25	26
27	28	29	30			

December
M	T	W	T	F	S	S
				1	2	3
4	5	6	7	8	9	10
11	12	13	14	15	16	17
18	19	20	21	22	23	24
25	26	27	28	29	30	31

1990

January
M	T	W	T	F	S	S
1	2	3	4	5	6	7
8	9	10	11	12	13	14
15	16	17	18	19	20	21
22	23	24	25	26	27	28
29	30	31				

February
M	T	W	T	F	S	S
			1	2	3	4
5	6	7	8	9	10	11
12	13	14	15	16	17	18
19	20	21	22	23	24	25
26	27	28				

March
M	T	W	T	F	S	S
			1	2	3	4
5	6	7	8	9	10	11
12	13	14	15	16	17	18
19	20	21	22	23	24	25
26	27	28	29	30	31	

April
M	T	W	T	F	S	S
30						1
2	3	4	5	6	7	8
9	10	11	12	13	14	15
16	17	18	19	20	21	22
23	24	25	26	27	28	29

May
M	T	W	T	F	S	S
	1	2	3	4	5	6
7	8	9	10	11	12	13
14	15	16	17	18	19	20
21	22	23	24	25	26	27
28	29	30	31			

June
M	T	W	T	F	S	S
				1	2	3
4	5	6	7	8	9	10
11	12	13	14	15	16	17
18	19	20	21	22	23	24
25	26	27	28	29	30	

July
M	T	W	T	F	S	S
30	31					1
2	3	4	5	6	7	8
9	10	11	12	13	14	15
16	17	18	19	20	21	22
23	24	25	26	27	28	29

August
M	T	W	T	F	S	S
		1	2	3	4	5
6	7	8	9	10	11	12
13	14	15	16	17	18	19
20	21	22	23	24	25	26
27	28	29	30	31		

September
M	T	W	T	F	S	S
					1	2
3	4	5	6	7	8	9
10	11	12	13	14	15	16
17	18	19	20	21	22	23
24	25	26	27	28	29	30

October
M	T	W	T	F	S	S
1	2	3	4	5	6	7
8	9	10	11	12	13	14
15	16	17	18	19	20	21
22	23	24	25	26	27	28
29	30	31				

November
M	T	W	T	F	S	S
			1	2	3	4
5	6	7	8	9	10	11
12	13	14	15	16	17	18
19	20	21	22	23	24	25
26	27	28	29	30		

December
M	T	W	T	F	S	S
31					1	2
3	4	5	6	7	8	9
10	11	12	13	14	15	16
17	18	19	20	21	22	23
24	25	26	27	28	29	30

Emergency Numbers

Police 000
Fire 000
Ambulance 000
Local police station _____
Nearest hospital _____
Doctor _____
Dentist _____
Chemist _____
Vet _____
Garage _____
Plumber _____
Electricity _____
Gas _____
Water Board _____

Mum and Dad _____
Baby-sitter _____
Hairdresser _____
School _____
Business _____

Frequently called numbers
_____
_____
_____
_____
_____
_____

	1991		

January
M T W T F S S
   1 2 3 4 5 6
7 8 9 10 11 12 13
14 15 16 17 18 19 20
21 22 23 24 25 26 27
28 29 30 31
	February
	M T W T F S S
	         1 2 3
	4 5 6 7 8 9 10
	11 12 13 14 15 16 17
	18 19 20 21 22 23 24
	25 26 27 28
		March
		M T W T F S S
		         1 2 3
		4 5 6 7 8 9 10
		11 12 13 14 15 16 17
		18 19 20 21 22 23 24
		25 26 27 28 29 30 31
			April
			M T W T F S S
			1 2 3 4 5 6 7
			8 9 10 11 12 13 14
			15 16 17 18 19 20 21
			22 23 24 25 26 27 28
			29 30

May
M T W T F S S
   1 2 3 4 5
6 7 8 9 10 11 12
13 14 15 16 17 18 19
20 21 22 23 24 25 26
27 28 29 30 31
	June
	M T W T F S S
	           1 2
	3 4 5 6 7 8 9
	10 11 12 13 14 15 16
	17 18 19 20 21 22 23
	24 25 26 27 28 29 30
		July
		M T W T F S S
		1 2 3 4 5 6 7
		8 9 10 11 12 13 14
		15 16 17 18 19 20 21
		22 23 24 25 26 27 28
		29 30 31
			August
			M T W T F S S
			        1 2 3 4
			5 6 7 8 9 10 11
			12 13 14 15 16 17 18
			19 20 21 22 23 24 25
			26 27 28 29 30 31

September M T W T F S S 30 1 2 3 4 5 6 7 8 9 10 11 12 13 14 15 16 17 18 19 20 21 22 23 24 25 26 27 28 29	**October** M T W T F S S 1 2 3 4 5 6 7 8 9 10 11 12 13 14 15 16 17 18 19 20 21 22 23 24 25 26 27 28 29 30 31	**November** M T W T F S S 1 2 3 4 5 6 7 8 9 10 11 12 13 14 15 16 17 18 19 20 21 22 23 24 25 26 27 28 29 30	**December** M T W T F S S 30 31 1 2 3 4 5 6 7 8 9 10 11 12 13 14 15 16 17 18 19 20 21 22 23 24 25 26 27 28 29